Religion, Science, and the Search for Wisdom

Proceedings of a
Conference on
Religion and Science
September 1986

David M. Byers
Editor

Bishops' Committee
on Human Values
National Conference
of Catholic Bishops

The primary goal of the NCCB Committee on Human Values is to establish ongoing dialogue between the bishops and the American scientific community. In keeping with this mission, the Committee hereby issues the proceedings of a Conference on Religion and Science held at St. John's Provincial Seminary, Plymouth, Michigan, September 15-18, 1986. The text was edited by Dr. David M. Byers, Executive Director of the NCCB Committee on Human Values Secretariat, and is authorized for publication by the undersigned.

Monsignor Daniel F. Hoye
General Secretary
NCCB/USCC

March 30, 1987

Excerpts from *"Gaudium et spes"* in *Documents of Vatican II*, Walter M. Abbott, SJ, General Editor, Copyright © 1966, America Press, Inc., 106 West 56th Street, New York, N.Y. are reprinted with permission. All rights reserved.

Scriptural excerpts in this book are from *The New American Bible*, copyright © 1970, Confraternity of Christian Doctrine, Washington, D.C., and are used with the permission of the copyright owner.

ISBN 1-55586-157-1

Contents

Preface / 1

Introduction / 3

Religion, Science, and the Search for Wisdom
   Most Rev. James A. Hickey, Speaker / 10

Natural Science and Belief in a Creator
   Rev. Ernan McMullin, Speaker / 14
   Discussion / 42

Science and Religion
   Dr. Freeman J. Dyson, Speaker / 48
   Rev. Paul M. Quay, SJ, Respondent / 63
   Discussion / 72

Religion and Evolutionary Theory
   Dr. Edward O. Wilson, Speaker / 82
   Rev. Thomas M. King, SJ, Respondent / 91
   Discussion / 95

Human Wisdom and Divine Wisdom
   Most Rev. Edmund C. Szoka, Speaker / 104

The Science-Values Relation: Impact of the Consciousness
Revolution
   Dr. Roger W. Sperry, Speaker / 110
   Rev. Joseph A. Bracken, SJ, Respondent / 119
   Discussion / 124

Faith and Science
  Dr. Jerome J. Lejeune, Speaker / 136
  Rev. Benedict Ashley, OP, Respondent / 149
  Discussion / 154

The Relationship between Science and Religion
  Dr. Ian G. Barbour, Speaker / 166
  Discussion / 184

Appendix I
  Committee on Human Values Statement of Purpose / 193

Appendix II
  List of Conference Participants / 195

Appendix III
  About the Speakers / 203

Preface

Presenting the proceedings of a conference in written form requires balance. One does not want to lose the sense of spontaneity and interaction that marked the meeting. On the other hand, people speak much more diffusely than they write. In order to produce a book that presents its subject coherently and without waste of words, sentences have been pared, material has been organized and rearranged, and conversational by-play that distracts from the orderly flow of ideas has been deleted. For example, the introductions and thank-yous, important as an expression of courtesy at the conference, are not reproduced here.

Of the eight central chapters of the book, six are amalgams. The centerpiece of each of these chapters is a major presentation. This address is followed by a formal response, floor discussion, or a combination of both. For easy reference, the names of the principal speaker, the presiding bishop, and the respondent (if any) appear on the half-title page of the chapter.

Chapter one consists of the welcome and opening remarks of Archbishop James Hickey, chairman of the Committee on Human Values. Chapter five is a homily that Archbishop Edmund Szoka of Detroit, in whose diocese the conference was held, delivered at a Mass celebrated for the conference participants.

On behalf of the Committee on Human Values, I would like to thank the speakers and respondents, who generously donated their time and talents in response to the bishops' invitation to discuss issues of basic importance to religion and science. Thanks are also due the Knights of Columbus, whose grant underwrote the conference itself and enabled the publication of these proceedings. Finally, a special word of gratitude to Patricia D. Boman, who was chiefly responsible for organizing the conference and who transcribed the tapes upon which, in large part, the present book is based.

David M. Byers
Editor

Introduction

As early as 1971, there existed a Secretariat for Human Values as part of the Bishops' Committee on Ecumenical and Interreligious Affairs. This secretariat served as a point of contact between the National Conference of Catholic Bishops (NCCB) and various institutes and think tanks across the country. It concerned itself primarily with the theological implications of such scientific/technological developments as the introduction of in vitro fertilization.

In 1974, the Vatican Secretariat for Non-Believers asked that each national episcopal conference establish a unit corresponding to the secretariat. In response, the NCCB set up the Committee on Human Values. The committee's task was to serve as a listening post vis-à-vis American science and culture. It would have a theological/philosophical rather than a sociological/political orientation. The committee would understand "human values" as a common ground on which to interact with scientists and those who professed no transcendental values. Bishop Mark Hurley, then of the Diocese of Santa Rosa, was elected first chairman.

The committee was staffed from 1975 to 1979 by an NCCB secretariat and underwent a change in direction. It tried to keep the bishops abreast of scientific advances. It also entered the public arena, insisting on the relevance of moral values in applying scientific discovery and technological know-how. During these years, the committee concerned itself with a wide range of issues including bioethical matters, recombinant DNA research, genetic engineering, human experimentation, environmental deterioration, and nuclear energy.

NCCB budget restrictions made the maintenance of a secretariat impossible after 1979. Nevertheless, Human Values remained in existence, and Archbishop James Hickey of Washington, D.C. was elected chairman in November 1984. He obtained part-time staff assistance and led the committee in evaluating its position. From this examination came a decision to reemphasize the committee's original purpose: to be the point of contact between the Church

and the American scientific community. The members felt, moreover, that religion and science are in tension. It is implicit in American culture that *science* is the only way of knowing; *scientific humanism*,
therefore, powerfully undermines religious faith.

Dialogue offered an opportunity to bring about a rapprochement
of religion and science. It is also the only practical way of establishing a proper theological basis for ethical analysis of thorny sci-
entific/technological issues. The committee decided to make
dialogue with the scientific community its primary goal, referring
particular ethical questions (e.g., on genetic engineering or the
environment) to other NCCB committees or outside agencies. Its
Statement of Purpose, finalized in September 1986, declares:

> The communication thus established [i.e., through dialogue] is of
> the highest value. Both religion and science have insights to share
> on the great philosophical and practical questions of our time. Cath-
> olic theology must confront the spirit of scientific humanism in con-
> temporary American culture, and Catholic moral values must be
> brought to bear on issues in science and technology. Wisdom lies
> where the truths of religion and science conjoin.

The Conference on Religion and Science held at St. John's Provincial Seminary in Plymouth, Michigan, September 15-18, 1986,
was the first step in establishing this ongoing dialogue between the
Catholic bishops and the scientific community. It was designed to
probe the tension between religion and science. The committee
invited as speakers four scientists eminent in their own fields and
known to have philosophical interests extending beyond science.
Freeman Dyson is a distinguished physicist whose book on the
arms race, *Weapons and Hope*, won a National Book Critics Circle
Award. Jerome Lejeune opened new fields for medicine by identifying the cause of Down's Syndrome in a chromosomal abnor-
mality. The work of Nobel laureate Roger Sperry has spurred much
investigation into the relationship of brain to mind. Finally, Edward
Wilson has established a new branch of biology—sociobiology—
and earned a Pulitzer Prize for his book *On Human Nature*.

To complement these scientists, the committee chose Rev. Ernan McMullin of the University of Notre Dame as keynote speaker.
Father McMullin is perhaps the best-known Catholic writer and
lecturer on the history and philosophy of science. Dr. Ian Barbour,
physicist, clergyman, and author of the standard text *Issues in Science*

and Religion, agreed to offer a summation and reflection at the close of the conference.

Four Catholic priests were invited to respond to the scientist speakers. Rev. Benedict Ashley, OP, has published recently a substantial volume entitled *Theologies of the Body*, which deals with some of the central questions in the relationship of religion to science. Rev. Joseph Bracken, SJ, seeks ways to accommodate science and religion through use of the process philosophy of Alfred North Whitehead. Rev. Thomas King, SJ, is an expert on the thought of Teilhard de Chardin and a founding member of Cosmos and Creation, a group of (mostly) Catholic scientists interested in the religion/science problem. Finally, Rev. Paul Quay, SJ, educated both as physicist and philosopher, has explored modern spirituality in *The Christian Meaning of Human Sexuality* and many other writings.

Speakers, respondents, committee members, and consultants comprised about twenty of the eighty conference participants. The others were chosen in two ways. Archbishop Hickey issued invitations to all the bishops in the country. The committee then wrote to the presidents of twenty Catholic colleges and universities, asking them to nominate four members of their faculties with credentials in theology, philosophy, physics, biology, evolutionary theory, or psychology. The committee selected participants from the resulting list, trying to achieve as much balance as possible as regards academic discipline, geographical location, and sex. Since very few women were nominated, the last goal was not achieved fully. But the committee's principal purpose—to involve the Catholic intellectual community in the conference—was.

The bishops' strategy for the conference—if one may use that term—was a bit unusual. Reversing their normal role, they resolved to learn rather than to teach, letting the speakers set the issues to be discussed. The letter of invitation each speaker received suggests the following theme for his talk: "Is there a convergence of your discipline with religion? What are the conflicts and points of agreement, either in goals or methods?" The conference agenda was stated broadly: "We hope that discussion on this level will help clear the air so that neither the religious nor the scientific community is uncomfortable in the presence of the other, and the insights of both can be brought to bear on the great questions of our age." The specifics of the agenda were left to the scientists to supply.

They did not disappoint. Freeman Dyson offered a philosophical view of the religion/science tension that was essentially conciliatory.

In the process, however, he raised an issue that triggered as much controversy as any other at the conference: authority in matters of belief. Dyson put the matter succinctly: "The assertion of papal infallibility, even in questions of faith and morals having nothing to do with science, grates harshly upon the ear of a scientist. We scientists are by training and temperament jealous of our intellectual freedom. We do not in principle allow any statement whatever to be immune to doubt."

Edward Wilson led the next session. He set forth the strict materialist philosophy for which he is well known, declaring, furthermore, that religion and science lie on opposite sides of a great gulf: "Although many theologians and lay philosophers like to deny it, I believe that traditional religious belief and scientific knowledge depict the universe in radically different ways. At bedrock, they are incompatible and mutually exclusive." This provocative statement, suggesting a man much less flexible and open-minded than Wilson proved to be, offered ground for a lively exchange of opinion.

Roger Sperry took a position diametrically opposed to Wilson's, even to the point of echoing his very words: "Where religious belief and scientific belief formerly stood in direct conflict, to the point even of being mutually exclusive, one now sees promise for a new compatibility, perhaps even harmony." His talk set the stage for discussion of *reductionism* and *downward causation*, terms not particularly current in religious thought but of considerable interest for the physical and behavioral sciences.

Indeed, discussion among scientists was one of the conference's hallmarks. With the bishops playing a prominent, but largely silent, role, the scientist speakers and participants found themselves debating among themselves. A high point occurred after Dr. Lejeune's talk, in which he rejected the neo-Darwinian explanation of evolution: "How fatuous it is to pretend we know how an elephant evolved from a primitive mouse, when we still do not understand how a tadpole becomes a frog." Dr. Wilson responded, saying, "This is fun because it is beginning to turn into a lively scientific debate." Later, he added good-humoredly: "I must rise heartily to the defense of neo-Darwinian theory. The group will find me substantially more dogmatic and inflexible in this case than I was in the face of God." Archbishop Hickey said in his opening remarks that the conference was about big ideas. The scientists, with the able assistance of philosophers and theologians, debated big ideas with honesty and grace.

The conference process was straightforward. Each major presentation, including the keynote address and summation, was followed by a formal response, floor discussion, or both. Floor discussion itself took two forms: small-group discussion around tables and, subsequently, give-and-take among the group as a whole. Staff supplied questions for small-group work but emphasized that they were merely "starters." The participants were to engage in free-wheeling debate in an effort to identify the issues that cause friction between religion and science in modern American culture.

Time was also set aside to talk about the future of discussion between the religious and scientific communities. The committee announced that it intends to initiate a series of dialogues with scientists and asked the participants to suggest topics for the first dialogue. While no consensus was reached, comment tended to center on two broad subjects, one philosophical, the other more practical. The first, stated as "Religion and Science as Pathways to Truth," focuses on epistemology. Granted that science, theology, and philosophy all offer legitimate methods for discovering objective truth about reality, how may these different methods be brought to bear on a given problem so as to arrive at a mutually satisfactory resolution? The second, stated simply as "The Global Ethic," asks how religion and science can cooperate to ensure that humanity not only survives but survives nobly on Planet Earth.

In line with its overall purpose, the committee has chosen to start with the philosophical question. Seven bishops, seven scientists, and seven philosophers/theologians will convene twice a year for at least two years. Their deliberations will result in a publication that either resolves the question before them or describes the areas of agreement and disagreement they discovered in the course of their analysis.

It is hard to predict events beyond this first dialogue. Certainly, the practical issues must be faced. A global ethic is quite literally a matter of life and death for our race. Moreover, there is a range of questions that the conference hardly touched, questions having to do with particular articles of faith. How does one explain the Incarnation or the Resurrection or the Real Presence in terms acceptable to science? Does the transcendent God of tradition truly touch our lives? If so, how are we to understand this intervention? How shall faith be sustained and nourished in an age of science?

We must not shrink from questions like these, as difficult as they may prove. The goal of dialogue between religion and science must be more ambitious than fostering a grudging tolerance. It must lead to a full-hearted willingness to accept the reality of the other's insight, to modify and supplement one's own truth with the other's truth. In Archbishop Hickey's words: "Let us speak most freely and openly, in the conviction that not religion alone, not science alone, but religion and science together can make us wise."

RELIGION, SCIENCE, AND THE SEARCH FOR WISDOM

Opening Remarks to Conference Participants

SPEAKER
Most Rev. James A. Hickey
Archbishop of Washington
Chairman, Committee on Human Values
National Conference of Catholic Bishops

Most Rev. James A. Hickey

I am not a scientist but a pastor. Like most Americans, I have maintained a real interest in the astonishing scientific developments of our era. I cannot claim any profound philosophical or technical understanding of these developments. As a bishop and as chairman of the Bishops' Committee on Human Values, however, I have an ever-growing awareness of the importance of dialogue between the religious community and the scientific community.

My brother bishops and I esteem you as experts in your chosen fields, and we are anxious to listen to your insights. We want to learn more clearly how the Church's faith can shed light on the great questions to which you devote your research and reflection. We want to learn more clearly how your discoveries can shed light on our faith and our mission. This conference is an opportunity to explore those areas where our disciplines intersect and interact, no less than the areas where there is tension or misunderstanding.

When I accepted the chairmanship of the Human Values Committee two years ago, I knew that certain emerging technologies, particularly those collectively called *genetic engineering*, would challenge the Church's ability to make its moral wisdom relevant in the modern world. I was anxious to broaden my knowledge and relate it to my pastoral ministry.

It soon became clear, however, that the committee's task extends far beyond the ethics of applied science. The Human Values Committee was created in response to a request from the Congregation for Non-Believers in Rome. Its goal is to bring the Church into fruitful dialogue with the materialism and humanism so prominent in contemporary culture, currents of thought that draw largely upon the physical and behavioral sciences.

Some may ask "Why bother?" Religion and science have been traveling steadily diverging paths since Galileo's day and have arrived at an uneasy truce. If one sets aside the often naive evolution/creationism debate, there are few brush fires to put out. For the most part, the religious and scientific communities ignore one another, each intent on its own task.

That, of course, is the problem! Viewed from one perspective, the task of religion and science is the same: to give a meaningful description of reality. Scientists and religious teachers make statements about reality that they assert to be true, even if they qualify what "true" means. Since reality is one, and the assumptions upon which religion and science operate are different, the descriptions they supply also differ.

In the abstract, one can agree with Einstein that these descriptions cannot conflict because they deal with completely distinct aspects of reality: the scientific one with facts and their relationships; the religious with fundamental ends and values. Pope John Paul II has made the same point on a number of occasions. The plain fact, however, is that ordinary people blur these neat categories. In practice, the world views of religion and science are in constant tension. There may be no sound reason why belief in science should undermine religious faith, but daily experience convinces me that it does.

This tension reveals itself in many familiar ways. People are embarrassed to talk of God or life after death in public because such matters are beyond the scope of empirical proof. Fundamental Christian doctrines such as the Resurrection or the Real Presence of Jesus in the Eucharist are glossed over as contrary to the laws of nature. The statements of popes and councils on sexual morality, ranging from abortion to contraception, are dismissed as "conservative" and contrasted with "progressive" and "more scientific" views.

It is fair to say, I think, that the media tend to adopt a smug attitude toward organized religion, except perhaps as it touches social justice issues. This attitude affects public perceptions in a profound, if semiconscious way. In modern America, the serious Christian or Jew, the serious believer, is considered unsophisticated.

This presents us bishops with a pastoral problem. Our responsibility is the care of souls. If scientific humanism presents a challenge to faith, even an implicit one, we must do what we can to resolve the tension for the good of our people. We believe that our God is the God of wisdom, a God whom we know more intimately as our knowledge grows of the world he created and sustains.

We can develop a theology that carefully relates the findings of science to the truths of faith. Our teaching and preaching can also reflect a greater understanding of the world science presents, the real world where the Gospel must be proclaimed. As religious leaders, we must grapple with the moral questions that trouble our people now, in a language they are used to hearing.

Together scientists, philosophers, and theologians seek wisdom. *Wisdom* is a big word. So is *truth*, which I used earlier. But this conference is about big words and big ideas, ideas that permeate our culture and profoundly affect the way we define ourselves and the object of the human quest. Let us speak most freely and openly, in the conviction that not religion alone, not science alone, but religion and science together can make us wise.

NATURAL SCIENCE
AND BELIEF IN A CREATOR

PRESIDER
Most Rev. James A. Hickey
Archbishop of Washington
Chairman, Bishops' Committee on Human Values
National Conference of Catholic Bishops

SPEAKER
Rev. Ernan McMullin
Director, Program in History and Philosophy of Science
University of Notre Dame

DISCUSSION

Rev. Ernan McMullin

INTRODUCTION

My task is to introduce a very large topic to a rather special audience made up of two quite different groups. One, the bishops, is charged with the preservation and propagation of the Catholic faith in the dioceses committed to their care. The other, the professors, is responsible for the teaching of science to college students. What the two groups most obviously have in common is a commitment to teaching, to the communication of a specific way of understanding the world. Where they differ is most obviously in what they teach and in the kind of authority with which they teach it. What prompts our conference are the affinities as well as the differences. For the two sets of teachings cannot be entirely isolated from one another; it is in the end a single world of which each claims a measure of understanding.

Our theme, then, is the relationship between these two different modes of understanding, between religion and science. Immediately, however, I must begin to narrow this topic to a more manageable compass. I took part recently in a conference on religion and science in Bombay, where the emphasis, not surprisingly, was on Hindu religion. The choice of topics took me rather by surprise, although, on later reflection, I realize that I ought not to have been surprised. What concerned the speakers most was the status of consciousness in the world. Hinduism finds genuine reality only in consciousness. The phenomenal or the material world is the realm of illusion. It is by retreating from this illusory world into the self, through meditation and asceticism, that one may hope to find the Absolute.

In such a perspective, the topic of religion and science obviously prompts a very different set of questions from those one would expect to find discussed here in the West. We found ourselves asking such questions as these: Can the reality of consciousness as a separate and transcendent sort of activity be demonstrated scientifically? How is it to be understood in terms of recent science? What is the status of idealism in contemporary philosophy, since idealism has the closest affinities with a world view that so strongly stresses consciousness, mind, and spirit? Is there scientific evidence for such psychic phenomena as telepathy or for claims to survival after death? Is it, in principle, possible to construct a computer that could properly be said to be conscious or to think? These are not, I dare say, the questions that would first occur to the present audience.

I am not going to talk, then, about the supposed affinities between quantum physics and Eastern mysticism, of which we have recently been hearing so much. Were I to do so, I would argue that such books as *The Tao of Physics*[1] do an injustice both to physics and to mysticism. It does Eastern religion no service to construe quantum theory in subjectivist terms. And, it does Western religion even less service, since this kind of stress on the primacy of consciousness or of subjectivity was never characteristic of the Judaeo-Christian tradition. But, my point here is a simpler one: the enterprise of relating science and religion is very different, East and West. My concern here will be with the West and specifically with the Christian world view. That, I think, will be scope enough.

What kind of enterprise are we engaged in? Where does it belong? Is it jointly a matter of science and of theology, to be dealt with by scientists and theologians working from different starting points? That might seem to be the premise of this meeting, and it certainly is a widely shared perception of the matter. But, the task of interrelating science and religious belief is not just a scientific or a theological one; indeed, I would say that it is not primarily either a scientific or a theological one. Tracing the relationships between the two belongs more immediately to the provinces of history and of philosophy. One may ask how these relationships have changed over time, how each has influenced the other. Or, one might attempt to clarify the presuppositions of procedure or of principle that guide each, with a view to discovering their mutual implications. The questions are characteristically those of the historian and the philosopher, but, of course, they are posed by all who are concerned

---

[1]Fritjof Capra, *The Tao of Physics: An Exploration of the Parallels between Modern Physics and Eastern Mysticism* (Berkeley: Shambhala, 1975). For a critical review of this genre of literature, see Sal P. Restivo, "Parallels and Paradoxes in Modern Physics and Eastern Mysticism," *Social Studies of Science* (1978): 143-181.

with the answers and have something to contribute to them. These may be physicist or theologian, psychologist or sociobiologist, historian or philosopher.

To my mind, such questions raise the most complex interdisciplinary issues. Fortunately, we now have a literature of considerable sophistication to help us.[2] What a change from a century ago when the simplicities of such works as Andrew Dickson White's polemic *The Warfare of Science and Theology* set the tone of the discussion. Passions still run high, of course, and passion has a way of short-circuiting scholarship, as the current debates on "creation science" have all too often illustrated. Perhaps, scholarship is less easily short-circuited than it used to be; there is, for one thing, so much more of it around. At any rate, this is the scholarship I will draw upon.

As we shall see, theology and the natural sciences intersect in all sorts of ways and in the most unexpected places. But, there is one central issue to which all the others are, to my mind, subsidiary. As a first approximation, let me say that the sciences deal with the world and theology with God. (This is obviously an oversimplification, but let it pass for the moment.) The relations between science and theology ought somehow, then, to reflect the relations of world and God. Our question then can be simply put—but alas! not so simply answered. What is God's relationship with the world?

I am not going to try to answer directly, not right away at least. Instead, I will try to suggest how the Christian responses to that question have gradually developed and to note the part played by the sciences in this development. I say "responses" because there has been a tension from the beginning between two rather different ways in which the Christian might construe God's relation to the regularities of nature that scientists commonly take as their starting point.

JERUSALEM

Let us go back, by way of introducing this topic, to the centuries when, in one part of the Mediterranean world, the Hebrew writings

---

[2]See, for example, the superb collection of historical essays, *God and Nature*, edited by David Lindberg and Ron Numbers (Berkeley: University of California Press, 1966).

that would shape all later Western religion were in the process of formation and, in another part of that same world, the Greeks were groping toward notions of nature, of cause, of demonstration, that would, after two millennia of slow transformation, provide the matrix for what we have come to call the Scientific Revolution.

Biblical scholars would generally agree, I think, that the primary focus of the writings that together comprise the Hebrew Bible, the Old Testament of the Christians, is on salvation history, on Yahweh's covenant with Israel, and not on cosmology, on Yahweh's role as cosmic Creator. Indeed, it would seem that the biblical references to creation were a later development in the Israelites' slowly dawning realization as to whom the Yahweh who had led them out of Egypt really was.[3] We might easily be misled by the order in which the books of the Bible now appear into supposing that this was the actual order of their composition and that the two creation narratives with which the *Book of Genesis* opens were, thus, the first part of the Bible written and were, thus, intended to define the character of what would come after. Were this true, it might be plausible to make a case that the Bible was written as a sort of cosmic history, opening with an explanation of how it all began.

But, the creation narratives in *Genesis*, as far as we can tell, were written much later than the accounts of the Exodus and the histories of David and Solomon.[4] Indeed, the majestic first chapter of *Genesis* was not composed until after the bitter experience of the Babylonian exile in the sixth century B.C., long after the historical chronicles. These much older writings celebrate Yahweh, the One who chose Israel as his special possession, dearer to him than all other peoples.[5] They tell of a mutual promise between Yahweh and the people whom he favored, a promise often betrayed on the side of Israel but constantly renewed by the One who had first extended his arm on their behalf. This was the Lord who had led a disorganized group of slaves out of Egypt, and who had taken their side against their enemies and eventually confirmed them in the possession of

---

[3]"In Israel's faith, redemption was primary, creation secondary, not only in order of theological importance, but also in order of appearance in the Israelite tradition." Bernhard W. Anderson, "The Earth is the Lord's," *Is God a Creationist?* ed. Roland M. Frye (New York: Scribner's, 1983), p. 180.

[4]See Dianne Bergant and Carroll Stuhlmuller, "Creation According to the Old Testament," *Evolution and Creation*, ed. Ernan McMullin (Notre Dame: University of Notre Dame Press, 1985), pp. 153-175.

[5]Exodus 19:5.

the land he had promised them, a land from which, they were convinced, he had helped them dispossess the original inhabitants.

There is nothing cosmic in this story, quite the reverse. Yet, as it was told and retold, as generations of prophets and priests reflected on who their Yahweh must be, the story took on new dimensions. In perhaps the earliest direct statement of Yahweh's creation of the universe, Jeremiah wrote: "Thus says the Lord of hosts, the God of Israel: It was I who made the earth, and man and beast on the face of the earth, by my great power, with my outstretched arm; . . ."[6] and went on to speak of a "new covenant," a much broader one that recognized Yahweh as the giver of "sun to light the day, moon and stars to light the night," thus linking him not only with the people of Israel but with the entire cosmos.[7]

The dependence of the entire universe upon the mighty power of God first came to be celebrated in those ringing psalm verses that have echoed down the ages. In the most eloquent of the creation psalms, the writer addresses Yahweh:

> You have spread out the heavens like a tent-cloth;
>   you have constructed your palace upon the waters.
> You make the clouds your chariot;
>   you travel on the wings of the wind.
> You make the winds your messengers,
>   and flaming fire your ministers.
> You fixed the earth upon its foundation,
>   not to be moved forever;
> With the ocean, as with a garment, you covered it;
>   above the mountains the waters stood.
> At your rebuke they fled,
>   at the sound of your thunder they took to flight;
> As the mountains rose, they went down the valleys
>   to the place you had fixed for them.
>
> You made the moon to mark the seasons;
>   the sun knows the hour of its setting.
> You bring darkness, and it is night;
>   then all the beasts of the forest roam about;
> Young lions roar for the prey and seek their food from God.
> When the sun rises, they withdraw and couch in their dens.
> Man goes forth to his work
>   and to his tillage till the evening.

---

[6]Jeremiah 27:4-5.
[7]Ibid., 31:31-35.

> How manifold are your works, O Lord!
>   In wisdom you have wrought them all—
>   the earth is full of your creatures.
>
> They all look to you to give them food in due time.
> When you give it to them, they gather it;
>   when you open your hand, they are filled with good things.
> If you hide your face, they are dismayed;
>   if you take their breath, they parish
>   and return to their dust.
> When you send forth your spirit, they are created,
>   and you renew the face of the earth.[8]

The Yahweh of Mount Sinai is now the Lord of heavens and earth, responsible for making all thing be. What the psalmist announces is the dependence of all things on Yahweh, their utter fragility. Unless the Lord gave breath, creatures would immediately cease to be. Even the earth, sun, and moon, eternal as they seem, owe their existence to his will. The world does not stand of itself; it needs constant renewal. God's role as Creator is not just a first fashioning of things but a constant sustaining in existence.

It ought to be emphasized that the psalmists were not responding to a request for explanation. They did not write as they did in order to explain why the world is the way it is. When the psalmist said, for example, that Yahweh wrapped the earth with waters that overtopped even the mountains and then caused the waters to retreat to a reservoir made for them beneath the earth, he was not proposing an explanation of the present relation of earth and sea. He was simply taking a belief about the waters beneath the earth that the Hebrews shared with other peoples of the Near East at the time and was using it with poetic force to help make his real point, which was the dependence of all things on Yahweh.

The shattering experience of the fall of Jerusalem in 587 B.C. and the loss of the land that Yahweh had given deepened this sense of dependence, of the need for redemption by a forgiving Lord. The earlier easy confidence was gone. The writings of this time reflect the feeling of a collapse, a chaos over all the earth, and cry out to Yahweh as the One on whom all order depends, the One who first brought order from chaos. The opening chapter of *Genesis*, composed around this time, expresses confidence that the same Lord who has protected Israel from its beginnings as a people is

---

[8]Psalm 104:2-8,19-24,27-30.

the mighty Creator, the fashioner of heavens and earth. It retells the story of creation presented in the far older and more primitive account of the origins of man and woman that now stands as chapter two of *Genesis*, perhaps also drawing upon the creation stories of the Canaanites and of the other peoples with whom the people of Israel had had such intimate dealings.

The familiar opening lines of *Genesis* are not yet, however, the creation "from nothing" of later Christian tradition. Though the best translation is still disputed, there would be fairly general agreement that what God is said to do is to bring order to something preexistent, namely, a waste of earth and waters. "When God set about to create the heavens and the earth, the earth was a formless void, there was darkness over the deep, and God's spirit hovered over the waters."[9] And when the work of creation, of bringing order to this chaos, is done, the waste of waters still exists, surrounding the inhabited earth on all sides, held back only by the power and goodness of God. Were it not for this power exerted as gift, chaos would return.[10]

Much more should be said, but I will have to summarize. The central theme of the Old Testament is the covenant between Yahweh and Israel, the covenant that, for the Christian, is finally sealed in the life and death of Christ. The awareness that one can see growing among the Israelites that the earth is the Lord's complements this earlier and more formative conviction. Israel's spokesmen, the prophets and leaders who brought this conviction into clearer and clearer focus, were not trying to explain anything. The creation narratives were not written as a cosmology but as an affirmation about the identity of the One who had redeemed them from the land of Egypt and who still sustained them. The warrant for these narratives, if one may use a notion that would have been alien to the writers themselves, was the continuing encounter of Israel with Yahweh. What they had learnt, what they had been helped to realize, was that not only they, but everything in the heavens and on earth, depends utterly on God. They had come to appreciate, as their Near Eastern neighbors had not, the gulf that separates Creator and creature. Remember God's powerful reminder to Job and, through him, to all creatures:

---

[9]David Kelsey, "The Doctrine of Creation from Nothing," *Evolution and Creation*, p. 186. Kelsey's entire discussion (pp. 176-196) is of interest.

[10]See Genesis 7:11;8:2.

Where were you when I founded the earth?
    Tell me, if you have understanding.
Who determined its size; do you know?
    Who stretched out the measuring line for it?
Into what were its pedestals sunk,
    and who laid the cornerstone,
While the morning stars sang in chorus
    and all the sons of God shouted for joy?

Have you ever in your lifetime commanded the morning
    and shown the dawn its place
For taking hold of the ends of the earth . . . ?[11]

The lesson could not be mistaken: God and God alone can give order to the morning; he alone can mark the boundary of the seas and set the stars in their courses. He entirely transcends his world; he is in no way part of it, though everywhere present in it. There is not the slightest suggestion that God can be identified with any power that is immanent in nature, as the other creation-stories of the Near East had implied.[12] Nature itself, indeed, is his gift; it is not to be taken for granted but must be seen as contingent, as something that might not have been. Though Yahweh had sometimes been presented in very human terms in the earlier writings—in his dealings with the first man and woman, for example—the *Book of Job* leaves us in no doubt that Yahweh lies beyond all human naming. Yet, it also conveys that there is still much we can say, and it is what Israel has darkly known from the beginning: that the God who holds all things in existence is, incredibly, a Being to whom his creatures can confidently look for redemption.

ATHENS

I want to switch scenes now and move across the Mediterranean in order to bring out a striking contrast, a contrast (to use a time-honored phrase) between Athens and Jerusalem. The biblical writers showed little or no interest in the causal explanation of natural process. But, the Greeks were fascinated by it and constructed speculative, but highly ingenious, accounts of how water or fire or atoms in motion might explain the diversity of kinds and changes they observed in the world around them. They took the world itself

---

[11]Job 38:4-7;12-13.
[12]"The Earth is the Lord's," p. 184.

as a given. Even though they might speculate about cosmic origins, their world was a solid one and the only origins they considered were natural transformations of one kind of material into another. Some of them saw traces of mind working with cosmic process, others did not. And those who did would, on occasion, link it with the "Divine." But, this was a very different notion of the Divine from that of the Hebrews. The Divine was needed in order to explain natural process, that was all. It was immanent within the process and, thus, accessible to the same sort of reasoning as was any other aspect of nature.

Greek natural science attained its height with Aristotle. He created whole fields such as physics, theoretical astronomy, logic, and, above all, biology—his first love and lifelong passion. Usually unemotional in laying out argument, he once introduced a work on physiology by speaking of the "immense pleasure" felt by "all those who can trace the links of causation," and went on:

> We must not recoil in childish aversion from the examination of humbler animals. Every realm of nature is marvelous . . . so we should venture on the study of every kind of animal without distaste, for each and all will reveal to us something natural and something beautiful. Nature's works exemplify, in the highest degree, the conduciveness of everything to an end, and the resultant end of Nature's generations is a form of the beautiful.[13]

The scientist of today would find no difficulty, I think, in recognizing and identifying with the spirit that animated those lines. Aristotle's sense of wonder, his admiration for nature in all its complexity, the excitement he so evidently felt in discovery—these assure us that natural science as we know it was already on the way. What would he and Jeremiah have had to say to one another? Not very much, I suspect. A separation was beginning to open between two very different ways of addressing the world, a separation later to become a gulf.

Aristotle was not an irreligious man. Indeed, if reverence for the natural world suffices to qualify a person as "religious," in that broader sense of the term often endorsed today, he could be called "religious." In the chapter from which I have already quoted, he notes that "of things constituted by nature, some are ungenerated, imperishable and eternal" and are, thus, "excellent beyond com-

---

[13]*On the Parts of Animals*, Book I, ch. 5; 645a 10-75.

pare, and divine."[14] These are, of course, the celestial bodies, animated by intelligence and moving in their unchanging circular orbits. The evidence from sensation—the only source of evidence Aristotle allows—that we have concerning them is scanty. Thus, there is little that we can know with certainty about them. But, this knowledge, limited though it may be, gives us "more pleasure than all our knowledge of the world in which we live, just as a half-glimpse of people we love is more delightful than a leisurely view of other things."[15]

Is there a hint here of religion, in the more familiar sense, involving love and worship? I think not. Note that he situates these beings among the things "constituted by nature"; they are as much a part of the world as the humbler animals whose study he also extolls. What sets them above these others is only the character of their motions; since these motions are circular and, thus, return on themselves, they are, in principle, eternal. There is a department of natural science devoted to the celestial bodies, the highest beings in Aristotle's world. And, the eighth and last book of his massive work *On Physics* terminates in the famous proof of the existence of a First Mover, itself unmoved. The First Mover is required, he argues, in order to explain how motion—any motion—occurs. It is an indispensable part of the physical order, though itself pure actuality, without any liability to change, and therefore is consequently immaterial.

If Aristotle speaks of "love" in this context, it is of a purely intellectual sort, of the kind he would also have had (and, one suspects, in greater measure) for the sea creatures he so painstakingly describes. Aristotle's universe is entirely self-contained, capable of being fully understood in human terms. This is naturalism in as clear a form as it has ever taken. There is no mention of a power on whom man depends for his being, nor of One to whom he may turn in worship or in prayer. In his works on ethics, Aristotle showed remarkable insight into the varieties of moral weakness, but the notion of sin, of an action that is wrong because it offends a loving God, is entirely absent. Aristotle's world, in short, was in many ways remarkably like that of many scientists today.

There were differences, of course, and I want to underline one of these. Aristotle argued that there could be science, real science,

---

[14]Ibid., 644b 23-25.
[15]Ibid., 644b 34—645a 1.

only of the *necessary*. Knowledge, at its best, would have to be unchanging, definitive. (Once again, note the preoccupation with changeability as defect.) For a true science of nature to be possible, the regularities of nature would themselves have to be necessary in character. In principle, one would have to be able to say that the essences of things could not be other than they are. Otherwise, explanation would still be incomplete.

Demonstration took on a quite technical meaning in this system, influenced, as it very likely was, by the axiomatic geometry just then beginning to be perfected. To demonstrate was to move from premises, themselves seen on intuitive grounds to be unquestionably true, to conclusions that followed deductively. It is a demanding notion, obviously. And one of the oddities of Aristotle's writings, which has prompted much discussion, is that demonstrations in this austere sense are few and far between in his own abundant work in natural science. His legacy is thus an ambiguous one: he requires the science of nature to be demonstrative, even though demonstrations appear to be very hard to come by. And, to sustain such a science, the operation of nature itself has to be necessary, inexorable. Chance events, it is true, can occur when lines of causality intersect. Acorns may be eaten by pigs and, thus, never attain their natural end of becoming oak trees. But, if they are given the proper environment, they necessarily become oak trees. Nature not only operates with necessity when not impeded, but it could not in the first place be other than it is.

I hope you will forgive this excursion into what might seem like irrelevant detail. But, you may perhaps have grasped already that a collision is now inevitable: Jeremiah and Aristotle cannot go their separate ways. Some day those ways will cross, and their descendants will be forced to join the battle. But, before we come to that dramatic moment—now ancient history since it occurred some seven centuries ago—I must return first to the world of Jeremiah or, rather, to the world he prepared. I have not, after all, said anything about Christianity. What did it contribute? Remember that the thread we are following is God's relationship to the world of nature.

AUGUSTINE

As we saw a moment ago, the doctrine of God as Creator came only gradually into focus across the centuries as the Israelites struggled to understand the Protector to whom they had been bound by covenant from their beginnings as a people. The notion of God's action as a creation "from nothing" (that is, an act of absolute bringing to be and not just a making from preexistent matter) is hinted at in a passage in the last historical writing of the Old Testament, The Second Book of Maccabees,[16] and again in The Epistle of Paul to the Romans.[17] But, it took firm shape in the first centuries of the Christian era in part, at least, in response to the prevalent dualisms of the day that represented matter as evil or, at least, as resistant to God's action.

What ruled these dualisms out for the Christian was above all, perhaps, the central affirmation that God had redeemed his world by entering into it and taking on the reality of a man, Jesus of Nazareth. It was no longer possible to allow matter some sort of independent existence prior to God's act of creating. It too had to be entirely dependent on God's act since Jesus had taken on the full materiality of human existence. As the story of redemption, which had begun to unfold in Israel and had come to a mighty climax in the life and death of Jesus, was internalized in the prayer and reflection of the Christian community, the conviction deepened of the absolute transcendence of the God on whom the universe depends and, yet, of his entrance into time in the person of Jesus and his continuing action within the world symbolized by the Spirit whom Jesus had promised would always be present. The doctrine of the Trinity thus meant a new and far more complex understanding of God's relationship to the world. It was not posited as a means of explaining otherwise inexplicable physical phenomena. Its warrant lay in the Scriptures and, ultimately, in the long revelation of God that had taken place across the centuries in the life of ancient Israel as well as in that of the new Israel announced by Christ.[18]

It was Augustine who finally brought the linked doctrines of Creation, Incarnation, and Trinity into clear focus. He is, in a way, the key figure in my entire story. I will have to discipline myself to be brief, since there is so much that could and should be said.[19]

---

[16]2 Maccabees 7:28.

[17]Romans 4:17.

[18]"The Doctrine of Creation from Nothing," pp. 184-92.

[19]For a fuller discussion, see Ernan McMullin, "Evolution and Creation," *Evolution and Creation*, pp. 9-16; and R. A. Markus, "Augustine," *Cambridge History of Later Greek and Early Medieval Philosophy*, ed. A. H. Armstrong (Cambridge: Cambridge University Press, 1967), pp. 395-405.

Augustine argued that Divine creation is a far more radical relationship than mere making from materials already there. It is a total
bringing to be, an act whereby the very existence of the world and
of each thing in the world is affirmed and sustained. God himself
cannot be part of nature, as Aristotle's First Mover was. Nor can
he, without contradiction, be said to create himself.

Since time is a condition of the creature, it too must be created
in the act whereby the world itself is brought to be. The Creator
himself is, thus, outside temporal process. He brings past, present,
future (these are our terms as creatures) to be in a single act. Creation
is not just something that happened a long time ago when all of a
sudden things began. It is also an action that at this moment sustains
all things in being. We must understand, says Augustine, that "God
is working even now, so that if His action should be withdrawn
from His creatures, they would perish."[20] This is the insight that
the psalmist had long ago expressed, but now it has been sharpened.
God does not act in the world by influencing in a special way the
causal processes accessible to us. Rather, he brings all to be in a
single act within which we can identify temporal and causal connections. The intelligibility we thus discover is a reflection of the
Divine Mind.

Let me recall for a moment Jacques Monod's *Chance and Necessity*.[21] Monod believes he is somehow undercutting a theistic understanding of cosmic process by excluding the directive operation
of mind within that process, as part of the process. Augustine's
immediate response would be that chance and necessity are equally
God's instruments. God achieves his purpose by bringing about
the mutations and the random encounters in the same act whereby
he brings about the regularities we interpret as "necessary." For
God, there are no chance events; he knows the future not by
knowing the present and inferring what will happen next but in
the same act by which he knows present and past (always remem-
bering that the terms *past, present,* and *future* reflect only the perspective of the created being). He brings about his ends not as a
mind that directs cosmic process from within, so to speak, but as
the Creator of the process, that is, the One responsible for there
being a process in the first place.

---

[20] *The Literal Meaning of Genesis*, trans. J. H. Taylor (New York: Newman, 1982),
I, p. 171.

[21] Jacques Monod, *Chance and Necessity* (New York: Knopf, 1971).

Several other features of Augustine's thought are worth recalling. He argued that the Genesis account of creation in six days could not have been meant as literal history. How could there be days, in the literal sense, before the sun was created? Yet, the sun appears on what is called in the text the fourth "day." Further, the term *day*, in its usual sense, is relative to one's position on the earth; when it is day in one part of the earth, it is night in another. The six "days" of the Genesis account, however, involve the entire earth. Augustine concludes that, clearly, the term must be taken metaphorically and goes on to speculate what the significance of the choice of the "seven-day" metaphor might have been.

Augustine uses a principle here that Galileo was to call on vainly in his own defense a thousand years later. Augustine asserts that if there is a conflict between a literal reading of Scripture and a well-established truth about nature, this of itself is sufficient reason to take the scriptural passage metaphorically. There cannot be a contradiction between nature and Scripture since God is speaking to us in both. This principle of exegesis is remarkable in that it allows natural science a role in determining the proper sense of Scripture. I say "remarkable" because Augustine emphasizes elsewhere that no one should worry if Christians are ignorant of the work of those he calls the "physicists" regarding the natures of things; it is enough for Christians "to believe that the cause of all created things, whether in the heavens or on the earth, whether visible or invisible, is nothing other than the goodness of the Creator, who is the one and true God."[22] Yet, even though Augustine ranks natural science far below the knowledge of God, he allows it enough firmness to make it significant, even for the interpretation of Scripture.

How, then, did the universe begin, in his view? God made all things together and, with them, time itself began. In that first instant, the seeds of all that would come later were already present; there would be no need for later addition. Even Adam and Eve, our first parents, were already present in potency in the materials from which the cosmos would gradually develop. One of his predecessors, Gregory of Nyssa, had already said the same thing: that a God who is truly Creator, not just a shaper of preexistent materials, would endow his creation from the beginning with all it needed to

---

[22]*Enchiridion*, adapted from the trans. by Albert Outler, *Library of Christian Classics* (Philadelphia: Westminster Press, 1955), p. 342.

carry out his ends. Gregory said in a wonderfully expressive passage: "The sources, causes, potencies of all things were collectively sent forth in an instant, and in this first impulse of the Divine Will, the essences of all things assembled together: heaven, aether, star, fire, air, sea, earth, animal, plant—all beheld by the eye of God."[23]

Gregory added that, because nature requires time and succession, the natures that were implanted in causal potency in that first instant would unroll only later in an order already implicit from the beginning. This was the famous doctrine of "seed-principles," which Augustine would later develop, and which was so often referred to by Christian defenders of the theory of evolution in those first decades after Darwin when evolution still seemed problematic from the Christian standpoint. However, Augustine's theory, strictly speaking, was not an evolutionary one since, for one thing, the natural kinds developed not from one another in a sequence over time but each from its own proper seed-principle when the circumstances of environment were right.[24] Augustine puts it this way: "All things were created by God in the beginning in a kind of blending of the elements, but they could not develop and appear until the circumstances were favorable."[25]

In those "seeds," as Augustine graphically calls them, there were "invisibly present" not only sun, moon, and stars but even the immense diversity of living things that required only, in addition to the seeds, the causal properties of water and earth.[26] What is striking about all this is Augustine's conviction that nature is complete in its own order. It does not need to be supplemented, adjusted, or added to. He allows, of course, for the occurrence of miracle, noting that it is not, as is commonly said, contrary to nature, only contrary to our human expectations.[27] Nothing can happen that is strictly contrary to nature. The "nature" of each thing, he says (and here his definition departs sharply from that of Aristotle), is "precisely what the supreme Creator of the thing willed [it] to

---

[23]"Apologetic Treatise on the Hexemeron," *Patrologia Graeca*, ed. J. P. Minge, 44, col. 72; quoted in E. C. Messenger, *Evolution and Theology* (New York: Macmillan, 1932), p. 24 (translation modified).

[24]This is discussed more fully in McMullin, "Evolution and Creation," pp. 11-16.

[25]*De Trinitate*, III, 9.

[26]*Literal Meaning of Genesis*, V, 23; 175.

[27]See David Lindberg, "Science and the Early Church," *God and Nature*, pp. 37-38.

be,"[28] which might, on occasion, include departures from the order we normally observe.

Augustine effectively distinguished between two orders of cause or explanation; each is complete in itself, but each also complements the other in a distinctive way.[29] We do not reach God through gaps in the natural order, through the inability of natural science to explain certain phenomena. God is "cause" not as part of the natural order, not as intervening here and there to bring things about that otherwise would not happen, but as primary creative cause of the entire natural order, as the agent responsible for its existence and its entire manner of being. It is one thing to call on God, who alone builds and governs creatures from the summit, Augustine reminds us; it is quite another to explain why things happen as they do in the natural order. For the latter, it is sufficient to refer to the capacities God has woven into the texture of the world from its first appearance.[30]

The natural world is a sign of God—Augustine has much to say, in consequence, about the nature of signs—because it is his handiwork and, therefore, reflects his purposes. God can, as it were, be seen through it.

> I asked the heavens, the sun, the moon, and the stars. "We are not the God whom you seek," said they. To all the things that stand around the doors of my flesh I said, "Tell me of my God. . . ." With a mighty voice they cried out, "He made us!" My question was the gaze I turned on them; the answer was their beauty. . . . Is not this beauty apparent to all men whose senses are sound and whole? Why, then, does it not speak the same to all men?[31]

This is, of course, the crucial question. Are not the invisible things of God "recognized through the things he has made," as Paul insists?[32] How, then, can it be that some simply do not see? Though

---

[28]*City of God*, XXI, 8, trans. Gerald Walsh and Daniel Honan, *Fathers of the Church* (Washington: Catholic University Press, 1954), p. 362.

[29]It would be an exaggeration to say that he made these distinctions entirely clear. There are hesitations in his exposition, and the view will only be worked out in its fullness by his successors. But, the essentials of it are there in Augustine, and this is what I want to stress here. See McMullin, "Evolution and Creation," p. 15.

[30]See Frederick Crosson, "Cicero and Augustine," to appear.

[31]*The Confessions of St. Augustine*, trans. John K. Ryan (New York: Doubleday, 1960), p 234.

[32]Romans 1:20.

the world may present the same appearance to the unreflective as
to the reflective, Augustine remarks:

> It is silent to one, but speaks to the other. Nay, rather, it speaks to
> all, but only those understand who compare its voice taken in from
> the outside with the truth within them. Truth says to me: "Your
> God is not heaven or earth or any bodily thing."[33]

God is not to be seen in the universe, then, but through it. And,
the seeing is not a matter of natural science but requires an attending
on the part of the individual to the truth that lies within himself
or herself, within his or her own history. This, indeed, is what *The
Confessions* was intended to illustrate, as Augustine reflected on his
own life in the light of the insight that all things come from God's
hands.

HOW COULD A CHRISTIAN BE AN ARISTOTELIAN?

In introducing the topic of religion and science, I have not chosen
to begin, as I might have done, with a review of the present state
of the question. My belief is that, in complex intellectual issues
like the present one, it is best to get a feel first for how it has all
come to be. Otherwise, one may easily take the contingencies of
the present mode of framing and addressing the question too seriously. Or, one may miss ambiguities or presuppositions that were
long ago laid bare in the historical record.

It simply won't do, of course, to end the story back in the fifth
century with Augustine. I will have to content myself with mentioning the first two great confrontations between Christianity and
the natural science that Augustine saw as complementary to it. The
first of these came in the thirteenth century in the new universities
of Western Europe—it had happened earlier in Islam—as the "natural works" of Aristotle (that is, his works on natural science) became
available in translation for the first time. Within a few decades,
they had become standard fare for Arts students in all the universities, notably in the two most renowned, Oxford and Paris. In
scope and detail, these works had no rival. Plato's *Timaeus*, which
had been the handbook for so long, was swept aside. The natural

---

[33]*The Confessions*, p. 235.

science taught in the universities to all students, including theology students, was by the mid-1200s that of Aristotle.

But, from the beginning an uneasiness manifested itself among the theologians. Aristotle's world was, after all, not a created world. It depended on nothing other than itself for its existence. Aristotle's science took the world as a given and, what was more, assumed its structure to be a necessary one. Indeed, the notion of scientific demonstration, as Aristotle elaborated it, seemed to depend on this. The status claimed for the truths of Aristotelian physics presupposed that the world of nature could not be other in kind than it is. How, then, could a Christian be an Aristotelian? Natural science and Christian belief began to seem incompatible. The freedom of God in his act of creation, fundamental to the Christian understanding, appeared to be excluded by the basic structure of Aristotelian science. Further, there were difficulties about specific doctrines such as the eternity of the world and the immortality of the human soul.

The university teachers of natural philosophy made heroic efforts to reconcile their Aristotelian teaching with Christian doctrine. Two young friars, Roger Bacon in Oxford and Thomas Aquinas in Paris, were especially creative in that regard. But, the theologians of Paris—the dominant school of theology in Europe—were, for the most part, unpersuaded, and they exerted pressure on the Church to ban the dangerous new views. In 1277, three years to the day from the untimely death of Thomas Aquinas, the Bishop of Paris condemned 219 propositions drawn indiscriminately from a variety of Aristotelian works, including those of Aquinas.

Lately, historians of science have been arguing about whether this condemnation marked a turning point in the history of science. I am not sure that the condemnation itself was as influential as has sometimes been claimed. It did no more than reinforce objections that had been fully formulated years before. The main issue was the necessitarianism underlying the entire Aristotelian notion of science, which seemed to compromise fatally the Christian doctrine of God's freedom in creating.[34] Some of the Christian upholders of this freedom went so far as to challenge the entire Aristotelian framework of nature and essence and to insist on the priority of the individual. They held that the way names are given to kinds

---

[34]See Edward Grant, "The Condemnation of 1277, God's Absolute Power, and Physical Thought in the Late Middle Ages," *Viator* (1979), pp. 211-244.

of things, as though they have in common something called a *nature* or *essence* or *form*, is merely conventional. Denying essence meant that knowledge could be gained only of the singular; generalizations could, at best, only be probable. No demonstrations of the Aristotelian kind were valid, since there were no essences to be known in the way Aristotle supposed.

This new and controversial stress on the individual (what came to be called *nominalism* among philosophers) was thus associated with a corresponding stress on the absolute freedom of God in the creating of each individual (what came to be called *voluntarism* among theologians). Lately, historians of science have spent so much time on an episode that hardly seems relevant to their interests since at least some of them are convinced that this stress on the primacy of the knowledge of the singular led to a novel conception of inductive science that was the immediate antecedent of—some have even said necessary condition for—the new science of Bacon and Descartes.[35] The matter is still disputed. There have been, to my mind, some manifest exaggerations on the part of historians who claim that the origins of modern science lie in the Calvinism they see as the inheritor of both the nominalism and the voluntarism of the fourteenth century. But, it does seem fair to say that in this instance Christian theology may have served as a corrective, a needed corrective, for Greek science. It is also worth celebrating one occasion, at least, when a bishop showed himself uncommonly perspicacious in regard to the presuppositions of scientific method!

Even though he was among those touched by the condemnation of 1277, Aquinas was not to stay in disfavor for long. Even before he was canonized in 1323, his mode of "Christianizing" Aristotle was widely accepted, and, indeed, Aristotle was well on his way to becoming "the Philosopher" for Christians. By 1346, Pope Clement VI could reprove those teachers and students at the University of Paris who showed a lack of respect for the "time-honored writings" of Aristotle, whose text, he said, should be followed "so far as it does not contradict Catholic faith."[36] What a dramatic change in only a few decades!

---

[35]See, for example, R. Hooykaas, *Religion and the Rise of Modern Science* (Grand Rapids: Eerdmans, 1972).

[36]Cited by Etienne Gilson, *History of Christian Philosophy in the Middle Ages* (New York: Random House, 1955), p. 471.

When arguing for the utility to the Christian of Aristotelian doctrines, Aquinas singled out the proof of an Unmoved Mover from the *Physics* as the "more manifest" way to prove the existence of a Being whom all Christians would understand as God. He went on to draw further on the resources of Aristotle's natural philosophy to construct several other alternative proofs, setting five of these at the celebrated opening of his principal work, the *Summa Theologiae*.[37] There could, after all, be no more effective way to demonstrate the orthodoxy of Aristotelian natural philosophy from the Christian standpoint than to show that it could be made the basis for a multiple affirmation of the existence of God.[38]

The first objection to this procedure was obvious, however. How could one possibly identify the Unmoved Mover of Aristotle with the Creator God of Augustine? The Unmoved Mover is at the end of a series that can be traced upward from every single motion; each member of the series reduces from potency to act, that is, moves the member immediately beneath it. By moving the outermost sphere, the Unmoved Mover in one version of the proof sets off a downward chain of cause-and-effect that terminates ultimately in the movements on earth that we perceive. But, this does not sound in the least like the action of a Creator. It is not as the first (or last) step in a long sequence that the Creator works but as the immediate cause of every member of the sequence, holding each equally in being. Yet, Aquinas appears to follow Aristotle in implying that without the Unmoved Mover the science of motion, physics, would be incomplete.

The argument to an Unmoved Mover depends on a fundamental principle of Aristotle's physics: "whatever is in motion is being moved by something other than itself," which is itself based on a conceptual analysis of the notions of potency and actuality. The

---

[37]Part I, q. 2, a. 3.

[38]Only the first of the five "Ways" is drawn directly from Aristotle; the third is inspired by Avicenna, while the fourth is neo-Platonic in concept. Gilson remarks that Aquinas is drawing here on philosophies that are, at bottom, inconsistent with one another. Averroes, for example, maintains that the existence of God can be proved only through physics; hence, for him, the proof from motion is the only valid one. Avicenna, on the other hand, insists that the proof must be metaphysical. Gilson argues that Aquinas took these different "Ways" from the works of natural philosophy but transformed them in the light of his own distinctively Christian understanding of the notion of efficient cause. See Etienne Gilson, *Elements of Christian Philosophy* (New York: Doubleday, 1959), pp. 80-87.

argument also assumes a hierarchy of movers; thus, it implicitly excludes the possibility that "A" might move "B" while "B" moves "A." The fifth "Way" likewise depends upon Aristotle's analysis of motion, specifically on the teleological directedness he took to be basic to the explanation of change. Natural bodies, Aquinas says, act always or nearly always in the same way so as to bring about the best outcome, that is, they act for an end. And yet, they lack any power of conscious planning on their own account. So, they must be constantly directed by a being with intelligence. In this case, there does not appear to be an intervening hierarchy of causes between the Designer and the natural motions of the elements. The assertion of the Designer's existence seems, however, to belong once again to physics. The Designer is to be held responsible for continuously goal-oriented motion on the part of bodies incapable of purpose or conscious desire.

Conceived as flowing from Aristotle's natural philosophy, these proofs may prove vulnerable in one or another of at least three ways. First, there may be logical flaws in the proofs themselves;[39] second, if the natural philosophy from which they derive is abandoned, the proofs fall; third, the Mover to which they conclude does not much resemble the Creator of the Christian tradition. Gilson and many other modern commentators on the "Ways" argue that they have to be extracted from the matrix of Greek natural philosophy and formulated in metaphysical language, utilizing a broadened existential notion of efficient cause that leads to the affirmation of a First Cause and not just an Aristotelian Mover or Platonic Demiurge.[40] In this way, they believe, the weaknesses of the original formulations can be overcome. The "Ways" then reduce, in a sense, to a single proof, one that begins from some observed general feature of the physical world such as motion or efficient causal relationship and argues to the necessity of a First Cause for the existence of such a feature. Gilson is at some pains to present the proofs, even the first Way, as being "independent of any scientific hypothesis as to the structure of the universe."[41] Whether, in the end, such a transformation is possible while re-

---

[39]Anthony Kenny has summarized the critical case against the Five Ways considered as logical demonstrations of God's existence. See *The Five Ways* (Notre Dame: University of Notre Dame Press, 1980).

[40]*Elements of Christian Philosophy*, p. 85.

[41]Ibid., p. 67.

taining the logical structure of the original proofs may be questioned. There can be no doubt, in any case, that Aquinas himself saw the proofs as being rooted in natural philosophy.

The importance of all this for us today is that, with the revival of the work of Aquinas in the nineteenth century, the "Five Ways" took on the character almost of an inspired text for Catholic apologists.[42] Claims that the existence of God could be readily "demonstrated" nearly always referred back to the five favored proofs. And, their cosmological character supported the assumption that the proper way to justify the rationality of the Christian belief in God is to begin from some specific feature of the natural world (such as motion or adaptation) that "science alone can never explain."

The consequences have been, in many ways, lamentable. The proofs have been detached from their original complex context in Aquinas's theology and made to look as though they could serve as they stand, as autonomous and entirely conclusive demonstrations. It has not been difficult for teachers of introductory college courses in philosophy to show the inadequacies of the proofs when they are taken in this way. Indeed, it would not be a great exaggeration to say that an indictment of Aquinas's logic has become a standard part of the formation of philosophy students at many American universities.

CONTEMPORARY NATURAL SCIENCE AND BELIEF IN A CREATOR

It is a long stretch from Aquinas's day to our own, and much could be said about how the discussion of religion and science has changed

---

[42]The noted Thomist author, Fernand Van Steenbergen, tells of the crisis that a paper of his, which was mildly critical of the logic of the Five Ways, caused at the 1950 International Thomist Congress in Rome. The paper merely argued that Aquinas's proofs had to be reformulated to make them cogent for the modern reader. But, even this implicit criticism was enough to elicit outrage. The encyclical *Humani Generis* had just appeared and was repeatedly invoked against those who would tamper with the venerable text of the Five Ways. So closely had this text become associated with Catholic orthodoxy that, as Van Steenbergen drily remarks, "the shadow of the Holy Office hovered over the assembly." *Dieu Cache* (Louvain: Presses Universitaires, 1961), p. 169.

over those centuries. One development would be particularly worth chronicling if space permitted: the rise of "physicotheology" in the seventeenth century. The claims to explanatory completeness of the "new science" of Galileo and Descartes led some, such as Boyle and Newton, to insist that natural science itself points to certain features of nature where God's direct intervention, outside the ordinary regularities of nature, has to be invoked. The analogy between physicotheology and the natural theology of the Thomist tradition is unmistakable, although there were important differences between them. The former, for one thing, laid more stress on the notion of a "gap" in the "regular" scientific accounts; the newly self-conscious natural science had drawn lines that made this boundary between the "regular" and the nonstandard much better defined than it had been in the time of Aquinas.

Physicotheology became a dominant motive for religious belief among intellectuals in the two centuries that followed but was undermined and ultimately destroyed by the scientific advances of the nineteenth century, especially Darwin's theory of evolution. The "gaps" did not remain gaps. And, even when they did, the "Filler of the Gaps" was hard to identify with the Creator God of the Christian tradition.

There are traces of physicotheology in many recent discussions of the role of God in evolutionary process. Teilhard de Chardin, for example, divides the energies that propel the world forward in time into two radically different sorts, tangential and radial. Only tangential energies are accessible to the methodology of conventional natural science. To explain the evolutionary process itself, he argues, one must introduce a "radial" energy that is basically psychic in nature and whose operation can be discerned only by employing a mode of understanding, a special "seeing" of pattern, which is very different in character from the modes of inference ordinarily recognized in biology. In this view, neo-Darwinian theory cannot, in principle, explain the forward thrust of evolution; it can handle only quantitative detail, not the qualitative advances. If the evolutionary process is carefully scrutinized in all its amplitude, the causal operation of mind-line energies will be discovered within it. These can be understood only by recognizing them as the manifestation of a creative Mind acting within the process, steering it toward goals set in advance. This orthogenetic and mentalistic reading of evolution has been immensely controversial. Needless to say, it has not been well received by neo-Darwinian theorists, who rightly see in it a basic rejection of their explanatory claims.[43]

Did Teilhard intend *The Phenomenon of Man* to serve the function of physicotheology? That is, did he think of it as a means of proving the existence of God, beginning from the facts of evolutionary change? It is hard to say. When he calls his system a "science," as he often does, he is implicitly asserting that there is an objective warrant for its theoretical claims, above all for the claim that the radial energies of the universe are the manifestation of a "hyper-personal Omega Point" toward which the universe is both ascending and converging. Teilhard sets the identification of this Omega Point with the Creator God of the Christian tradition in an epilogue, but even here "it is not the convinced believer but the naturalist who is asking for a hearing."[44] He seems to be saying that a science of cosmic evolution, if properly carried through, will end in an affirmation of the existence of a Being who is at once immanent and transcendent, spiritual and personal. Teilhard would not use the language of demonstration, but he would surely want his science to be seen as a means of raising people's vision to God.

By now, we know what the dangers are. First, the sciences of cosmic evolution, as they develop, will find no place for Teilhard's "within," for a psychic energy powering the universe in steady progress toward a preset goal. Second, the God discovered in this way can be no more than a world-soul, a cosmic mind, or the like. There does not seem to be any way to reach the transcendent God of Jeremiah and Augustine through a "science" based on the energies of cosmic evolution.

Where does this leave us? Do the natural sciences bear on belief in a Creator in any way today? There has been one intriguing recent development that is worth mentioning, even though an adequate treatment of it is beyond the scope of my presentation.[45] Until the

---

[43]For a recent sympathetic account of Teilhard's biology, see Edward O. Dodson, *The Phenomenon of Man Revisited* (New York: Columbia University Press, 1984).

[44]*The Phenomenon of Man* (New York: Harper & Row, 1959), p. 292.

[45]See my essay "How Should Cosmology Relate to Theology?" *The Sciences and Theology in the Twentieth Century*, ed. Arthur Peacock (Notre Dame: University of Notre Dame Press, 1981), pp. 17-51, especially pp. 40-46. For an exhaustive survey (though in some respects perhaps an exceedingly speculative one), see John Barrow and Frank Tipler, *The Anthropic Cosmological Principle* (New York: Oxford University Press, 1986).

early 1970s, cosmologists assumed that the kind of universe we have could originate from an initial state that did not need to be specified in any detailed way. Descartes had talked about an initial "chaos" of particles in motion out of which order gradually emerged, according to mechanical law. The details of this story proved far more difficult to fill in than Descartes or anyone in the seventeenth century could have anticipated, but, by the 1950s, it seemed as though a plausible story could be told, in outline at least.

In the mid-1960s, the "Big Bang" model received strong confirmation from the discovery of a pervasive microwave radiation of just the sort the model predicted. But, the application of elementary particle theory, and of quantum theory generally, to the first moments of the "Big Bang" gave a most unexpected result. It turned out that a "life-bearing" universe, one that would allow life to develop—the necessary conditions include the existence of elements heavier than hydrogen and helium, the formation of planets, and sufficient time for evolution to occur—is extremely unlikely. Estimates varied, but the Cambridge theorists who first developed these ideas (Hawking, Rees, Carr) assigned such a universe a probability of less than one in a million.

What do probability estimates mean in this context, when we have only one universe from which to work? The application of current physical theories to the first few seconds of existence of a "Big Bang" universe shows that a great many widely different lines of development are possible. However, almost none of them lead to a universe in which complex life could develop, so far as we can tell. The evolution of a life-bearing universe requires very precise constraints on the initial state; to use a metaphor, which has since become famous, this initial state must be "fine-tuned." The theories themselves do not limit the possible universes sufficiently, so the limitation must come from a very precise setting of the initial conditions.

A number of writers suggested that this limitation could be "explained" by adverting to the presence of human life in the universe, and, thus, the much-discussed "anthropic principle" was born.[46] The universe must be limited in certain ways; since if it were not, we would not be here! But, does this explain? To my mind, not

---

[46]The term was first used by Brandon Carter. See "Large Number Coincidences and the Anthropic Principle in Cosmology," *Confrontation of Cosmological Theory and Astronomical Data*, ed. M. S. Longair (Dordrecht: Reidel, 1974), pp. 291-298.

as it stands; some supplement is needed. Quite a number have been suggested. For example: the possibility that this is only one of a large number of existing "parallel" universes, in which case, it would become explanatory to say that we are in the only one we could be in.

But, the most obvious way to convert the anthropic principle into a properly explanatory (but no longer strictly "scientific") one is to suppose that the "fine-tuning" is the work of a Creator who, in some sense, "intends" life to develop in the way it did. The Creator would choose one among all the physically possible universes (recall: "possible" is used in reference to current physical theory); that it should be the life-bearing one is no surprise to the Christian!

What makes this form of the design argument attractive to many, apart from the credentials it claims in cosmology, is that it does not require any intervention, strictly speaking, on God's part. There is none of the alteration of causal lines that we saw in classical physicotheology. It is just a matter of God's choosing a certain sort of universe in the first place, the universe in which human life will "naturally" develop.

The argument, of course, still relies on a "gap," namely, the inability of contemporary physical theory to explain the original tight specification of the initial cosmic state. This has already proved to be the argument's main weakness. More recent developments, particularly of the so-called inflationary models of the initial cosmic expansion, have shown that the original puzzling, "unlikely" specification may be at least partially explicable in broader theoretical terms.[47] The issue is much debated, and it is far too early to say where the debate may lead. Moreover, other possibilities that would undermine the theological version of the anthropic principle must also be kept in mind: the possibility of life-forms quite different from anything we can presently imagine, for example.

This recent revival of the "design" type of natural theology is unexpected and raises a number of intricate philosophical issues. The argument is necessarily to a transcendent Creator, not to a world-soul or even an all-powerful Craftsman. The agent who brings the universe to be is not itself limited to that universe. The argument, however, is of the classical "design" type: it relies on the discovery of an apparent means-end relationship that cannot, or at

---

[47]See Alan H. Guth, "Inflationary Universe: A Possible Solution to the Horizon and Flatness Problems," *Physical Review D* (1981), pp. 347-356.

least apparently cannot, be explained in a nonteleological way. Even though the argument avoids many of the hazards of the older natural theology, its conclusion is, at best, a "consistency" one: a Being who "fine-tunes" the universe is consistent with the Creator God of the Christian tradition.[48]

Leaving aside this rather exotic alternative, where are we now in our quest? Two main alternatives seem to be open. One is to search for traces of mind within cosmic process (as many others besides Teilhard have done) and then identify that mind somehow with the Divine. Whitehead and others who have followed this track have labored to conceive the God of process as, at least in some sense, transcendent, but they inevitably suggest an identification between God and universe, portraying God as a Being striving toward self-realization through the cosmic process. The tension between this notion and the classic Christian conception is obvious, even though some theological support can be claimed for it. The tension between its idealism and the naturalism of modern natural science is equally evident.

The other alternative is the one that harks back to Augustine. It stresses the transcendence of God and the self-sufficiency, in "natural" terms, of the universe he created. This emphasis obviates the need to invoke a special not-quite-natural energy animating cosmic process. The "chance" and "necessity" of the evolutionary story have to be reinterpreted; they are such only in the eyes of the theorist. For the Creator, there is neither chance nor necessity, only a single act in which all comes to be.

The advantages of this standpoint are obvious.[49] It acknowledges the transcendence of God as Christians have most often understood it, and it allows for the immanence of a Creator who is present through his conserving power at every moment and in every place.

---

[48]Freeman Dyson, "The Argument from Design," *Disturbing the Universe* (New York: Harper, 1979), p. 251. In an essay that excited considerable controversy, Dyson reaches a carefully stated conclusion: "I conclude from the existence of these accidents of physics and astronomy that the universe is an unexpectedly hospitable place for living creatures to make their home in. Being a scientist, trained in the habits of thought and language of the twentieth century rather than the eighteenth, I do not claim that the architecture of the universe proves the existence of God. I claim only that the architecture of the universe is consistent with the hypothesis that mind plays an essential role in its functioning."

[49]For a recent defense of this "neutrality principle," as he calls it, see Howard J. Van Till, *The Fourth Day* (Grand Rapids: Eerdmans, 1986).

But, its disadvantages are by now also clear. The "wholeness" of creation means that it leaves no loose ends for the traditional sort of natural theology to tie up. There is, it would seem, no scientific approach to justifying the existence of a Creator of the sort described by Augustine. There are not gaps to fill; the Creator has seen to that!

We may, then, lack an argument for God's existence that would convince a science-minded generation. True, the existence of the universe—why it should be rather than not be—does not lend itself to scientific explanation and, yet, still seems to most a question that ought not to be disallowed on *a priori* grounds. But, natural science does not of itself lead to belief in a Creator, even though it does, for the believer, extoll the work of the Creator in ways the psalmist could never have imagined. The road from Athens does not lead to Jerusalem after all. But, the roads from Athens and Jerusalem may still lead in the same direction.

Discussion

ARCHBISHOP HICKEY: Although it was not on our schedule, Fr. McMullin has graciously agreed to take a few questions.

DR. JAMES WALTER: Fr. McMullin, your talk discusses the relationship between science and theology. This conference, however, is focused on science and religion. I don't see these as the same.

FR. MCMULLIN: One must distinguish the relationship between science and religion from that between science and theology. They clearly are not the same. The issues that set science apart from faith generally occur in the intellectual order of speculation, of explanation, of proof, which pertain much more to the world of theology than to the world of religion. I mentioned the broader context of religion when speaking of Greek thought. If one includes the believing community, worship, liturgy, tradition, and so on, one can easily move from the systematic articulation of theology to the set of practices and beliefs that animates this theology.

My principal concern here, however, is with theology, not Christian theology in general, but with what came to be called "natural theology." When scientists who are themselves believers—either Christians or simply theists—look within their own science for motives of belief, one has to be very wary about the conclusions they draw. The God one discovers by this method may not be the God of the Christian tradition. That difficulty surfaced long ago in the Aristotelian debates of the thirteenth century. At the end of each of his five arguments for the existence of God, Aquinas used the famous phrase, "and this all men call God." Yet, it isn't really what Augustine would have called God. Augustine was not thinking of God as an Aristotelian "Prime Mover," because his God had a much larger job. He was *not* a mover at the end of a sequence of movers.

I was trying to suggest, by emphasizing the biblical tradition, that the impetus to belief in a Creator ordinarily comes from something else other than abstract argument about some particular feature of the natural order. Further, Christians believe in a different sort of God—a Creator who sustains at all moments every aspect of the order. He does not enter into it as an explanation of some limited part of the order such as motion or design. God is responsible for motion—of course he is. He is responsible for design. But, no one should suppose that the Darwinian or any other explanation of design within the order of secondary causality is therefore incomplete. God cannot be "located" in the role of Prime Mover as the terminus of a purely physical argument.

ABBOT WALTER COGGIN: Aquinas's fourth proof—from perfection in the universe—refers to existence, while the first three deal with motion, the order of essences, and change. In the first three proofs, Aquinas shows that God is the ultimate cause of *change* in finite beings. In the fourth proof, he demonstrates God to be also the ultimate cause of the *existence* of finite, changing beings. In the fourth proof, Aquinas addresses himself to God as Creator, the giver of existence.

FR. MCMULLIN: I must admit I have a great deal of difficulty with the fourth way. In his short work "On Being and Essence," Aquinas makes a different suggestion. His real originality consists not in the distinctions he draws between matter and form, or the other dichotomies of the Aristotelian tradition, but between essence and existence. He would say, "There is a Being whose essence, so to speak, *is* existence." Metaphysical insights like that require no cosmological underpinning. It is the sort of argument that Aquinas's whole metaphysics stands or falls on.

I challenge the idea that the existence of God can be proved by arguing from some observable fact in the natural order, which can *only* be explained by invoking God as the beginning of a sequence. Proceeding that way puts God into the natural order. That is one thing Augustine insisted must *not* be done.

I haven't discussed the Christological dimension of this question. Of course, God *has* entered the natural order through the Incarnation. There is a great deal to say about how God enters the historical reality of our world through the contingencies of Bethlehem. Dealing with this and the sustaining presence of the Holy Spirit opens up the whole Trinitarian perspective. Historically, however, the primary focus for people engaged in the pursuit of science is the Creator God. Men of science who are also believers

have been tempted over the centuries to suppose that the only way
to prove the existence of the Creator is to take a scientific approach.
This seems to me an inevitably vulnerable way to proceed.

DR. WALTER: Natural theology has been criticized because it
seems to set God's action in the world against the laws of nature.
God is invoked to explain what nature cannot explain; he becomes
the "God of the gaps." Can the action of God in the moral order
run afoul of psychology in the same way? As knowledge increases,
could psychology fill moral gaps as physics filled physical gaps? We
could find ourselves in the twenty-first century where religious
theorists were in the sixteenth century, but facing the conclusions
of psychology.

FR. McMULLIN: I have been insisting upon the Augustinian
principle of God's sustaining action, of God's power as it reveals
itself in the free actions of human beings or the falling of stones.
God's sustaining presence as Creator in no way forbids the possibility of understanding these phenomena in scientific terms. Such
understanding depends on the extent to which the scientist can
discover regularities within natural process, regularities that can
function as the basis for causal explanations and ultimately theoretical explanations. If the scientist can so analyze moral action,
fine. This analysis may cause problems, but they are not problems
about our relationship with God. Even while recognizing the regularities the scientist points out, I would argue that God is present
in moral action.

DR. WALTER: Just as He would be present in physical action.
It seems, though, that psychologists and moral theologians have
divided the pie in the same way that cosmologists and natural
theologians did earlier. The psychologists' province is here, the
moral theologians' province there.

FR. McMULLIN: I really am not a moral theologian, for which
I constantly bless Providence. But, let me make one remark that
might be helpful. There is a set of issues in moral theology having
to do with determinism and freedom. If a scientist can find within
human action regularity sufficient to sustain a science, does this
undercut human freedom? No. In the same way, does God's action
as sustainer of moral action somehow defeat the attempt to understand it scientifically? I think not. These are two different kinds
of enterprise.

The enterprise of the scientist who attempts to find regularity
in the causal order does not consist in seeking necessities in the

Aristotelian way but, rather, in constructing theories that account for the phenomena. The scientific investigation of causation is really complementary to the theologians' insistence that everything in the natural order is sustained by God and sustained in the integrity of the original act of creation.

FR. JOSEPH BRACKEN, SJ: I became a little uneasy when you contrasted Athens and Jerusalem and questioned the use of science to prove the existence of God. In one way, I agree with you. I, too, am fearful of identifying God with a function within a metaphysical or scientific system, because that limits him. On the other hand, science is seen as the paradigm of reason in our society. If we do not create a system in which the interplay of God and the world is described in detail and which takes the best science and the best theology of the day into account, then gaps between faith and reason can open up. We can find ourselves believing in faith what we reject in reason. I would rather recognize the fallible character of the various systems from Aquinas on than implicitly accept "two truths."

FR. MCMULLIN: I could easily be tempted to suggest an addition to the scriptural passage where Christ faces three temptations; I would add a fourth: to offer scientific proof for the claim he was making for himself. It is a temptation to which we, over the ages, have too often succumbed. Although science is a paradigm of rationality in our world, it is simply not the only mode of rationality. We must resist the implication that all is lost unless we can find some gaps through which to stuff God into the scientific textbook. That temptation has been disastrous from the thirteenth century onward.

You mentioned the "two truths." Even though I have, in some sense, separated the domain of religious belief and the domain of science, there is another sense in which I have tried to unite them. Faith and reason address the same reality. When the theologian or the prophet speaks, it is the scientists' world he is talking about, not some other world. On the other hand, as Galileo knew, the conclusions of the scientists are relevant to what the theologians are saying. If Freud comes up with a satisfactory account that excludes the notion of human freedom, theologians had better take notice!

Teilhard de Chardin tried to show how the two truths complement one another. The details of Teilhard's system are, to my mind, inadequate. But he has rendered us immense service, and not just as a poet or mystic. Aquinas was hindered as a metaphysician by the apparent fact that God the Creator, in bringing his world to be, seems to pop everything in like unrelated items on a checklist. There is no cousinship, just mosquitos and elephants and stars, all different. That is not satisfactory, even from the Thomistic stand-point itself.

I can well imagine that Aquinas would have welcomed the kind of evolutionary insight Teilhard was able to bring. Teilhard sup-plements the theology and philosophy of Aquinas by showing how, within a single order of creation, the seeds of Augustine actually do come to be. It is a self-sufficient order, a creation after the proper fashion of a creator, not a creating of matter and a subsequent insertion of living beings like afterthoughts. Of course God *could* do that, but there is something deeply troubling about this notion of God, as many writers from Descartes's time onward were to point out. So, here is an instance of scientific theory completing Christian metaphysics and Christian theology or, at least, bringing it closer to completion.

One could go further and reiterate a point that Teilhard rightly makes much of: Incarnation means that God takes on, through a man, the nature of the world. What God becomes through Jesus of Nazareth is not simply a single human soul. The entire history of the universe made the son of Mary possible. In some sense, the entire physical universe is being raised up. We can go back with theoretical physicists, like Dr. Dyson, to those first moments, carry creation through the march of evolution with Dr. Wilson, and show how it all hangs together. When we speak, then, of God taking on human nature, we now have a much more rarified notion of human nature. The body and soul that Christ assumed took eons to fashion.

SCIENCE AND RELIGION

PRESIDER
Most Rev. Edward M. Egan
Auxiliary Bishop of New York

SPEAKER
Dr. Freeman J. Dyson
Professor of Physics
Institute for Advanced Study, Princeton University

RESPONDENT
Rev. Paul M. Quay, SJ
Research Professor in Philosophy
Loyola University (Chicago)

DISCUSSION

Dr. Freeman J. Dyson

I am grateful to the Committee on Human Values for asking me to come here to take part in your discussion of religion and science as a representative of the physical sciences. But, I must say at the outset that I speak for myself alone. I will not pretend to speak for my physicist colleagues. Still less do I speak for chemists and geologists and computer experts. Any statement that attempted to express a consensus of physical scientists about religious and philosophical questions would miss the main point. There is no consensus among us. The voice of science is a Babel of diverse languages and cultures. That is to me the joy and charm of science. Science is a free creation of the human mind, and, at the same time, it is an international club, cutting across barriers of race and nationality and creed. Many first-rate scientists are Catholics; many are Marxists; many are militant atheists; many are like me, loosely attached to Christian beliefs by birth and habit but not committed to any particular dogma.

Let me introduce my remarks with a story about a child. One thing that scientists and bishops ought to have in common is a reverence for children. When my son was three years old, he liked to crawl into my bed in the early morning and talk about the problems of life. One morning he said abruptly, "You know there are two Gods." I was surprised and asked him, "What are their names?" He replied, "One is called Jesus and he makes people, and the other is called Bacchus and he makes wine." I suppose my son must have picked up from his surroundings a certain tendency to polytheism. Anyone who has read or seen a performance of that intensely religious drama the *Bacchae* of Euripides will be aware that Bacchus is or was a formidable deity, making extreme demands upon his followers. In the tragedies and exaltations of the modern drug culture, Bacchus is alive. I doubt whether my three-year-old son was conscious of all this, any more than he was conscious of the fine points of the doctrine of the divinity of Jesus. His statement showed, in my opinion, a certain innate religious feeling, expressed in language appropriate for the child of a physicist. That is why I find it worth mentioning in the context of our discussion today.

Science and religion are two great human enterprises, sharing many common features. They share these features also with other great enterprises such as art, literature, and music. The most salient features of all these enterprises are discipline and diversity: discipline to submerge the individual fantasy in a greater whole; diversity to give scope to the infinite variety of human souls and temperaments. Without discipline, there can be no greatness. Without diversity, there can be no freedom. Greatness for the enterprise, freedom for the individual: these are the two themes, contrasting but not incompatible, that make up the history of science and the history of religion.

PHYSICS AND GEOGRAPHY

My own field of physics is passing today through a phase of exuberant freedom, a phase of passionate prodigality. Sometimes as I listen to the conversation of my young colleagues at Princeton, I feel as if I am lost in a rain forest, with insects and birds and flowers growing all around me in intricate profusion, growing too abundantly for my sixty-year-old brain to comprehend. But, the young people are at home in the rain forest and walk confidently along trails that, to me, are almost invisible. They have their own discipline, different from the discipline that I was taught forty years ago, but still as strict in its way as mine. They are not wandering aimlessly. They are explorers, mapping out the ground, finding the ways that will lead them out of the jungle up to the mountain peaks.

There is a curious parallel here between the history of physics and the history of geographical exploration. At the beginning, the explorers had their eyes on the mountain peaks. George Everest, the organizer of the geological survey of India, left his name on the highest mountain. The intervening jungles were only obstacles to be overcome. And, so it was also in physics. Maxwell's equations of the electromagnetic field, Einstein's theory of general relativity: these were the great mountain peaks that dominated our vision for a hundred years. But, God did not only create mountains, he also created jungles. And, today, we are beginning to understand that the jungles are the richest and most vibrant part of his creation. The modern explorers in South America or in Africa are not looking for mountains. They are looking into the depths of the jungles to observe and to understand the creatures who live there in all their intricate variety. We ourselves came out of the jungle a few million years ago, and we now are becoming aware that we need to understand and preserve the jungle if we are to remain alive and healthy on this planet.

Likewise, in physics, it turned out that God's creation was far richer than either Maxwell or Einstein had imagined. There was a time in the 1920s and 1930s when it seemed that the landscape of physics was almost fully mapped. The world of physics looked simple. There were the great mountains explored by Maxwell and Einstein and Rutherford and Bohr, the theories of relativity and the quantum, great landmarks standing clear and cold and clean in the sunlight, and between them only a few unimportant valleys still to be surveyed. Now, we know better. After we began to explore seriously the valleys in the 1950s, we found in them flora and fauna as strange and unexpected as anything to be seen in the valleys of the Amazon. Instead of the three species of elementary particle that were known in the 1920s, we now have sixty-one. Instead of three states of matter—solid, liquid, and gas—we have six or more. Instead of a few succinct equations to summarize the universe of physics, we have a luxuriant growth of mathematical structures, as diverse as the phenomena that they attempt to describe. So, we have come back to the rain forest, intellectually as well as geographically.

What are the philosophical lessons to be learned from the recent discoveries in physics, from the discovery that nature is as prolific in particles as in biological species? Here again, I do not speak for my colleagues but only for myself. In my opinion, the main lesson to be learned is that nature is complicated. There is no such thing as a simple material universe. The old vision that Einstein maintained until the end of his life, of an objective world of space and time and matter independent of human thought and observation, is no longer ours. Einstein hoped to find a universe possessing what he called "objective reality," a universe of mountaintops that he could comprehend by means of a finite set of equations. Nature, it turns out, lives not on the mountaintops but in the valleys.

Dr. Edward Wilson kindly sent me an advance copy of his talk. He is speaking as an evolutionary biologist. He speaks about two philosophical viewpoints that he calls *scientific materialism* and *religious transcendentalism*. Of them, he says, "at bedrock, they are incompatible and mutually exclusive." I will not begin now to criticize and contradict Dr. Wilson before he has had a chance to speak. I found his talk full of wisdom, and I agree with most of his conclusions. Only, I must say, speaking as a physicist and not as an evolutionary biologist, that I do not know what the word *materialism* means. Speaking as a physicist, I judge matter to be an imprecise and rather old-fashioned concept. Roughly speaking, *matter* is the way particles behave when a large number of them are lumped together. When we examine matter in the finest detail in the experiments of particle physics, we see it behaving as an active agent rather than as an inert substance. Its actions are, in the strict sense, unpredictable. It makes what appear to be arbitrary choices between alternative possibilities. Between matter as we observe it in the laboratory and mind as we observe it in our own consciousness, there seems to be only a difference in degree, not in kind.

If God exists and is accessible to us, then his mind and ours may, likewise, differ from each other only in degree and not in kind. We stand, in a manner of speaking, midway between the unpredictability of matter and the unpredictability of God. Our minds may receive inputs equally from matter and from God. This view of our place in the cosmos may not be true, but it is at least logically consistent and compatible with the active nature of matter as revealed in the experiments of modern physics. Therefore, speaking as a physicist, I say that *scientific materialism* and *religious transcendentalism* are neither incompatible nor mutually exclusive. We have learned that matter is weird stuff. It is weird enough so that it does not limit God's freedom to make it do what he pleases.

SCIENTIFIC HUMANISM

The letter of invitation to the speakers at this conference says: "The bishops are aware that scientific humanism represents an alternative to Christian faith, even if the opposition between the two is often left implicit. They seek ways of reconciling the divergent currents in our culture so as to be more effective teachers of their people."

I will try to be responsive to this request for a meeting of minds. I am not sure what *scientific humanism* means. I suppose a scientific humanist is somebody who believes in science and in humanity but not in God. If that is the correct definition, I do not quite qualify as a scientific humanist. I cannot regard humanity as a final goal of God's creation. Humanity looks to me like a magnificent beginning but not the last word. If I had to choose between humanity and God, I am not sure I would choose humanity. Small children often have a better grasp of these fundamental questions than grown-ups. It happened to me that I adopted a step-daughter. I moved into her family when she was five years old. Before that, she had been living alone with her mother. Soon after I moved in, she saw me naked for the first time. "Did God really make you like that?" she asked with some astonishment. "Couldn't he have made you better?" That is a question with which every scientific humanist should be confronted, at least once in a lifetime. The only honest answer is, of course, "yes."

My personal brand of scientific humanism is strongly influenced by the writings of H. G. Wells, and especially by Wells' *Outline of History,* a wonderfully lucid account of the history of mankind written in 1920. I give you some quotations from Wells, because I find his philosophy relevant to the theme of this conference. First, two sentences at the beginning to set the stage for his history: "Not only is Space from the point of view of life and humanity empty, but Time is empty also. Life is like a little glow, scarcely kindled yet, in these void immensities."[1] It was important for Wells, and for me, that the stage is very large and humanity is very small. An awareness of our smallness may help to redeem us from the arrogance that is the besetting sin of scientists.

Halfway through his history, when he comes to the life and teachings of Jesus, Wells puts in a paragraph addressed explicitly to the relation between science and religion:

> Though much has been written foolishly about the antagonism of science and religion, there is indeed no such antagonism. What all these world religions declare by inspiration and insight, history as it grows clearer and science as its range extends display, as a reasonable and demonstrable fact, that men form one universal brotherhood, that they spring from one common origin, that their individual lives, their nations and races, interbreed and blend and go on to merge again at last in one common human destiny upon this little planet amidst the stars. And the psychologist can now stand beside the preacher and assure us that there is no reasoned peace of heart, no balance and no safety in the soul, until a man in losing his life has

[1]H. G. Wells, *The Outline of History, Being a Plain History of Life and Mankind,* I (London: George Newnes, Ltd., 1920), p. 11.

found it, and has schooled and disciplined his interests and will beyond greeds, rivalries, fears, instincts and narrow affections. The history of our race and personal religious experience run so closely parallel as to seem to a modern observer almost the same thing; both tell of a being at first scattered and blind and utterly confused, feeling its way slowly to the serenity and salvation of an ordered and coherent purpose. That, in the simplest, is the outline of history; whether one have a religious purpose or disavow a religious purpose altogether, the lines of the outline remain the same.[2]

Perhaps the humanism of Wells sits more easily with religion because he was by nature an artist rather than a scientist. He was trained as a biologist, but he made his living as a writer. He cared more for the turmoil and travail of the individual human soul than for the biology of the human species. As a scientist, he knew that human passions and feelings—love and brotherhood and the fear of God—have a longer history and deeper roots in people's minds than science.

After the remarks that I quoted about the general relations between religion and science, Wells continues with the narrative of the life of Jesus, as it is told in the Gospels. And, then, he goes on to do something extraordinary, to add a couple of sentences that strengthen rather than weaken the power of the gospel story:

It was inevitable that simple believers should have tried to enhance the stark terrors of this tragedy by foolish stories of physical disturbances. . . . But if indeed these things occurred, they produced not the slightest effect on the minds of people in Jerusalem at that time. It is difficult to believe nowadays that the order of nature indulged in any such meaningless comments. Far more tremendous is it to suppose a world apparently indifferent to those three crosses in the red evening twilight, and to the little group of perplexed and desolated watchers. The darkness closed upon the hill; the distant city set about its preparations for the Passover; scarcely anyone but that knot of mourners on their way to their homes troubled whether Jesus of Nazareth was still dying or already dead.[3]

Wells was, of course, no Christian. He was, I suppose, a scientific humanist. But, he recognized in the life and death of Jesus, and in the subsequent rapid growth of the Christian Church, the great turning point of his outline of history. He recognized a transcen-

---

[2]Ibid., p. 364.
[3]Ibid., p. 365.

dental quality in these events, a spiritual force that overshadowed the political and social history in which they were embedded.

I quoted at some length from Wells because he is a prime example of a scientific humanist sympathetic to Christianity. He was sympathetic because his science left room for the transcendental. He was himself a preacher, preaching the moral regeneration of mankind through education. He was a revolutionary, believing in the evanescence of all earthly kingdoms. He stood firmly in the tradition of Christian millenarianism. He taught the coming of a future of hope and glory for humanity, just as Jesus taught the coming of the kingdom of Heaven.

Wells represents the version of scientific humanism that I find congenial. There are many other versions, some friendly to religion, some indifferent, some hostile. Science is not a monolithic body of doctrine. Science is a culture, constantly growing and changing. The science of today has broken out of the molds of classical nineteenth-century science, just as the paintings of Picasso and Jackson Pollock broke out of the molds of nineteenth-century art. Science has as many competing styles as painting or poetry. For better or for worse, science is a part of human nature, and human nature is irremediably diverse.

The diversity of science also finds a parallel in the diversity of religion. Once, when I was a child, walking with my mother through the English cathedral town of Winchester, I asked her: "Why are there so many different churches?" My mother gave me a wise answer: "Because God likes it that way. If he had wanted us all to worship him in one church, he would not have made so many different kinds of people." That was an answer invented on the spur of the moment to satisfy the curiosity of a five-year-old. Now, almost sixty years later, it still has the ring of truth.

I do not expect Catholic bishops to agree with my mother on this point. The Catholic Church has made a great and, on the whole, successful effort to find a place within one Church for a great diversity of people. Within the one Church were the Jesuit fathers O'Hara and Ward, whose textbook on projective geometry opened my eyes to the beauties of abstract mathematics; the physicist Father Yanase, who has been a cherished member of our Institute for Advanced Study at Princeton and is now at the Gregorian University in Rome; the best-selling literary Trappist monk Thomas Merton; and the heroic Mother Teresa of Calcutta. Nevertheless, I believe my mother was right. Not everybody who worships

God can or should be a Catholic. In the nature of God and in human nature, there is a far greater diversity of spirit than any one church can encompass, just as in the nature of the universe there is a far greater diversity of structure and behavior than any one discipline of science can elucidate.

DISCORD AND CONCORD

Broadly speaking, religion and science can live harmoniously together in the human soul so long as each respects the other's autonomy, so long as neither claims infallibility. Conflicts occur when organized science or organized religion claims a monopoly of truth. The ethic of science is supposed to be based on a fundamental open-mindedness, a willingness to subject every belief and every theory to analytical scrutiny and experimental test. In 1660, The Royal Society of London proudly took as its motto the phrase *Nullius in Verba*, meaning "No one's word shall be final." The assertion of papal infallibility, even in questions of faith and morals having nothing to do with science, grates harshly upon the ear of a scientist. We scientists are by training and temperament jealous of our intellectual freedom. We do not, in principle, allow any statement whatever to be immune to doubt.

On the other hand, as I listen to the arguments raging in recent years between biologists and creationists over the teaching of biology in American schools, I am shocked to hear voices among the biologists sounding as arrogant and intolerant as the voices of the creationists. In these arguments, the parents of schoolchildren are complaining that the public schools use taxpayers' money to destroy the religious faith of their children. The parents have a legitimate complaint. The tragedy of their situation lies in the fact that their religious beliefs are in genuine conflict with the evolutionary doctrines of modern biology. But, the biologists, by and large, show no respect or understanding for the human anguish of the parents. The biologists say with a tone of contempt: "Your religious beliefs are no concern of ours. There is only one right way to teach biology in schools, and we decide how to teach it because we are the experts and we know what is true." The biologists, in other words, are claiming to be as infallible as the pope. This is tragedy for both sides in the dispute. It is tragic for the parents to have their deep religious convictions overridden by a group of arrogant experts.

And, it is tragic for the biologists to present to the parents a false image of science, an image of intolerance and insensitivity, and thereby to raise a generation of citizens who consider science to be their enemy.

Of course, there is no easy solution to the conflict between fundamentalist Christian dogma and the facts of biological evolution. I am not saying that the conflict could have been altogether avoided. I am saying only that the conflict was made more bitter and more damaging, both to religion and science, by the dogmatic self-righteousness of the biologists. What was needed was a little more human charity, a little more willingness to listen rather than to lay down the law, a little more humility. Scientists stand in need of these Christian virtues just as much as bishops do.

The conflict between creationists and evolutionists is a sorry chapter in the history of science and religion. In such conflicts, the worst elements on both sides come to the fore. What begins as a simple human tragedy ends as a grotesque legal squabble in which lawyers on each side try to prove the other side wrong. The children, over whose hearts and minds the battle is fought, need to see that there is good on both sides, that both their parents' faith and the wider vision of science are worthy of respect. Instead, the children become pawns in a power struggle. No matter who wins, the bitterness of the struggle can only do them harm.

Fortunately, the battle over creationism involves only a small minority of religious believers and of scientists. Far more important is the vast area of social and political action within which religion and science are finding common concerns and opportunities for fruitful collaboration. Religion and science have one essential quality in common: both are truly international enterprises. Both are international not only in spirit but in the details of daily work and organization. Both stand opposed to the narrow and selfish nationalism that would cut them off from their international roots. Both see the human race as one. Both render unto Caesar the things that are Caesar's, but both reach around the world in the conviction that the essential core of human achievement and human dignity has nothing to do with Caesar.

In recent years, science and religion have come more and more into alliance through their common concern for peace. Our concern here is not the ethical problems of nuclear weapons and military strategy. But, I must say a word of thanks for the magnificent pastoral letter on war and peace, *The Challenge of Peace: God's Promise and Our Response*, which you bishops hammered out and issued to the world in 1983. That letter is indeed a challenge, a challenge to us scientists as well as to everybody else. It expresses a fundamental rejection of the idea that permanent peace on earth can be achieved with nuclear weapons. It challenges scientists to put our skills to work in more hopeful directions, in directions leading to peace and reconciliation rather than to a precarious balance of terror. As a scientist, I am also grateful for the initiatives that the Pontifical Academy of Sciences in Rome has taken recently, both to help and advise His Holiness the pope in his efforts to promote nuclear disarmament, and to heal the wounds created long ago by the trial and condemnation of Galileo.

FAITH AND REASON

But, it is time now to return to our main theme: the proper limits of faith and reason. I am now speaking of faith and reason not in the sphere of political action but in the sphere of personal belief. Here, even more than earlier, I speak only for myself. I am describing a private balance between faith and reason. I do not pretend that scientists, in general, think as I do. I state my conclusions merely as an example, to show you how one particular scientist thinks.

My own faith is similar to the faith of Wells. I believe that we are here to some purpose, that the purpose has something to do with the future, and that it transcends altogether the limits of our present knowledge and understanding. I do not wish to go beyond this simple statement into a discussion of theology. My ignorance of theology would quickly become obvious. If you like, you can call the transcendent purpose God. If it is God, it is a God inherent in the universe and growing in power and knowledge as the universe unfolds. Our minds are not only expressions of its purpose but are also contributions to its growth.

Like the majority of scientists in this century, I have not concerned myself seriously with theology. Theology is a foreign language, which we have not taken the trouble to learn. But, I did once have some help from a professional theologian in formulating my ideas in an intellectually coherent fashion. I happened to meet Charles Hartshorne at a meeting in Minnesota, and we had a serious conversation. After we had talked for a while, he informed me that my theological standpoint is Socinian. Socinus was an Italian heretic who lived in the sixteenth century. If I remember correctly what Hartshorne said, one of the tenets of the Socinian heresy is that God is neither omnipotent nor omniscient. He learns and grows with his creation. I do not pretend to understand the theological subtleties to which this doctrine leads if one analyzes it in detail. I merely find it congenial and consistent with scientific common sense. I do not make any clear distinction between Mind and God. God is what Mind becomes when it has passed beyond the scale of our comprehension. Whether or not this was what Socinus taught, it is what I mean when I use the word *Socinian*.

In the no man's land between science and theology, there are five specific points at which faith and reason may appear to clash. The five points are (1) the origin of life; (2) the human experience of free will; (3) the prohibition of teleological explanations in science; (4) the argument from design as an explanatory principle; and (5) the question of ultimate aims. Each of these points could be the subject of a one-hour lecture, but, fortunately, I have only a few minutes for all five. I will summarize each of them, in turn, as well as I can in the time available.

First, the origin of life. This is not the most difficult problem from a philosophical point of view. Life in its earliest stages was little removed from ordinary chemistry. We can at least imagine life originating by ordinary processes, which chemists know how to calculate. Much more serious problems for philosophy arise at a later stage with the development of mind and consciousness and language. The physicist Wigner once asked where in the Schrödinger equation one puts the joy of being alive. The problem with the origin of life is only this: How do you reconcile a theory that makes life originate by a process of chance with the doctrine that life is a part of God's plan for the universe? There are three possible answers to this question. Answer 1: Deny that God has a plan, and say that everything is accidental. This is the answer of Jacques Monod and of the majority of modern biologists. But, then, Wigner will ask: Is consciousness also an accident? Answer 2: Deny that chance exists, and say that God knows how the dice will fall. This is the answer of Einstein, who believed that chance is a human concept arising from our ignorance of the exact workings of nature. But, then, why do statistical laws play such a fundamental role in physics if chance is only a cover for our ignorance? Answer 3: Say that chance exists because God shares our ignorance. This is the answer of Hartshorne, the Socinian heresy. God is not omniscient. He grows with the universe and learns as it develops. Chance is a part of his plan. He uses it as we do to achieve his ends.

The second clash between faith and reason is the problem of free will. The problem is to reconcile the direct human experience of free will with a belief in scientific causality. Here, again, we have the same three alternative answers to deal with the conflict. But not both narrow-minded science and narrow-minded theology stand opposed to free will. The Jacques Monod view of the universe as pure chance and necessity denies free will. The orthodox theology of an omniscient and omnipotent God also denies it. For those of us who would like to believe both in God and in free will, the Socinian answer is the best way out. The philosophical problems of chance and of free will are closely related. The Socinian theology deals with both together. Free will is the coupling of a human mind to otherwise random processes inside a brain. God's will is the coupling of a universal mind to otherwise random processes in the world at large.

My third problem is that of forbidden teleology, the conflict between human notions of purpose and the operational rules of science. Science does not accept Aristotelian styles of explanation, that a stone falls because its nature is earthy and so it likes to be on earth, or that the human brain evolved because the nature of humanity is to be intelligent. Within science, all causes must be local and instrumental. Purpose is not acceptable as an explanation of scientific phenomena. Action at a distance, either in space or time, is forbidden. Especially, teleological influences of final goals upon phenomena are forbidden. How do we reconcile this prohibition with our human experience of purpose and with our faith in a universal power?

I make the reconciliation possible by restricting the scope of science. The choice of laws of nature and the choice of initial conditions for the universe are questions belonging to metascience and not to science. Science is restricted to the explanation of phenomena within the universe. Teleology is not forbidden when explanations go beyond science into metascience. The most familiar example of a metascientific explanation is the so-called anthropic principle. The anthropic principle says that laws of nature are explained if it can be established that they must be as they are in order to allow the existence of theoretical physicists to speculate about them. We know that theoretical physicists exist: ergo, the laws of nature must be such as to allow their existence.

This mode of explanation is frankly teleological. It leads to non-trivial consequences, restrictions on the possible building blocks of the universe, which I have no time to discuss in detail. Many scientists dislike the anthropic principle because it seems to be a throwback to a pre-Copernican, Aristotelian style of reasoning. It seems to imply an anthropocentric view of the cosmos. Whether you like the anthropic principle or not is of course a matter of taste. I personally find it illuminating. It accords with the spirit of modern science that we have two complementary styles of explanation: the teleological style, allowing a role for purpose in the universe at large; and the nonteleological style, excluding purpose from phenomena within the strict jurisdiction of science.

The argument from design is the fourth on my short list of philosophical problems. The argument was one of the classic proofs of the existence of God: the existence of a watch implies the existence of a watchmaker. This argument was at the heart of the battle between creationists and evolutionists in nineteenth-century biology. The evolutionists won the battle. Random genetic variations plus Darwinian selection were shown to be sufficient causes of biological evolution. The argument from design was excluded from science because it makes use of teleological causes. For a hundred years, the biologists have been zealously stamping out all attempts to revive the old creationist doctrines.

Nevertheless, the argument from design still has some merit as a philosophical principle. I propose that we allow the argument from design the same status as the anthropic principle, expelled from science but tolerated in metascience. The argument from design is a theological and not a scientific argument. It is a fundamental mistake to try to squeeze theology into the mold of science. I consider the argument from design to be valid in the following sense. The universe shows evidence of the operations of mind on three levels. The first level is the level of elementary physical processes in quantum mechanics. An electron in quantum mechanics is an active agent, constantly making choices between alternative possibilities according to probabilistic laws. Every quantum experiment forces nature to make choices. It appears that mind, as manifested by the capacity to make choices, is to some extent inherent in every electron. The second level at which we detect the operations of mind is the level of direct human experience. Our brains appear to be devices for the amplification of the mental component of the quantum choices made by molecules inside our heads. We are the second big step in the development of mind. Now comes the argument from design. There is evidence from peculiar features of the laws of nature that the universe as a whole is hospitable to the growth of mind. The argument here is merely an extension of the anthropic principle up to a universal scale. Therefore, it is reasonable to believe in the existence of a third level of mind, a mental component of the universe. If we believe in this mental component and call it God, then we can say that we are small pieces of God's mental apparatus.

The last of the five philosophical problems is that of final aims. The problem here is to try to formulate some statement of the ultimate purpose of the universe. In other words, the problem is to read God's mind. Previous attempts to read God's mind have not been notably successful. One of the more penetrating of such attempts is recorded in the book of Job. God's answer to Job out of the whirlwind was not encouraging. Nevertheless, I stand in good company when I ask again the questions Job asked: Why do we suffer? Why is the world so unjust? What is the purpose of pain and tragedy? I would like to have answers to these questions, answers that are valid at our childish level of understanding, even if they do not penetrate very far into the mind of God.

My own answers are based on a hypothesis that is an extension both of the anthropic principle and of the argument from design. The hypothesis is that the universe is constructed according to a principle of maximum diversity. The principle of maximum diversity operates both at the physical and at the mental levels. It says that the laws of nature and the initial conditions are such as to make the universe as interesting as possible. As a result, life is possible but not too easy. Always when things are dull, something new turns up to challenge us and to stop us from settling into a rut. Examples of things that make life difficult are all around us: comet impacts, ice ages, weapons, plagues, nuclear fission, sex, sin, and death. Not all challenges can be overcome, and so we have tragedy. Maximum diversity often leads to maximum stress. In the end we survive, but only by the skin of our teeth.

The expansion of life and of humanity into the universe will lead to a vast diversification of ecologies and of cultures. As in the past, so in the future, the extension of our living space will bring op-

portunities for tragedy as well as achievement. To this process of
growth and diversification, I see no end. It is useless for us to try
to imagine the varieties of experience, physical and intellectual and
religious, to which humanity may attain. To describe our metamorphosis as we embark on our immense journey into the universe,
God gave us the humble image of the butterfly. All that can be
said was said long ago by Dante in Canto Ten of the *Purgatorio*:

> "O you proud Christians, wretched souls and small,
> Who by the dim lights of your twisted minds
> Believe you prosper even as you fall,
> Can you not see that we are worms, each one
> Born to become the angelic butterfly
> That flies defenseless to the Judgment Throne?"

Rev. Paul M. Quay, SJ

As Dr. Dyson indicated at the beginning of his talk, "the main point" to see about scientists' attitudes toward religion is that these attitudes are endlessly diverse. "Many first-rate scientists are Catholics; many are Marxists; many are militant atheists; many are . . . loosely attached to Christian beliefs by birth and habit but not committed to any particular dogma."

It is not their science, then, that determines scientists' belief or lack of belief. They may well agree with one another about their science; their lack of agreement on religion must have some other source. Our physics can be used for a materialist's attack on religion or for a religious physicist's praises of God. Both types of persons are easily found today. What is important for our discussions is that it cannot be "the scientific world view," which they hold in common, that makes the vast differences between them.

Dr. Dyson more than once mentioned philosophy in the same breath with religion. I would like to strengthen their relationship and argue that philosophy is the formal medium of contact between science and religion. That is, only by using some (even if only implicit) philosophy can one use a scientific fact or theory to support or to damage a religious position.

Yet, more than philosophy is involved. The whole of one's culture clearly has some bearing on one's attitudes toward religion. Though, at times, people speak as if it were the science of a given period that determines its world view, I think that C. S. Lewis was closer to the truth in his "The Funeral of a Great Myth."[1] He contends that it is the myths of a period that give rise to much of its science or, at least, to the latter's characteristic forms. By *myth*, he seems to mean little else than "a story, the origin of which is forgotten, ostensibly historical but usually such as to explain some practice,

---

[1]C. S. Lewis, "The Funeral of a Great Myth," *Christian Reflections*, W. Hooper, ed. (Grand Rapids, Mich.: Eerdmans, 1967), pp. 82-93.

belief, institution, or material phenomenon,"[2] except that he would not require that its "historical" aspect be confined solely to the past. A good myth speaks also of the future. Lewis, then, shows that universal evolution existed in one form or another as a myth among the poets and artists a good half-century before the biologists got interested in it. Keats and Wagner contributed much that prepared the way for Darwin.

Something similar might be said concerning present-day myths of space exploration and colonization. Without science, they would be mere exercises of creative imagination. But, it is not science that gives them their power over the minds and hearts of those who are laboring already with vigor to bring them about in practice.

Because of scientists' wide diversity of views on philosophy and religion, and because religions differ far more from one another than the sciences do, I think it may be useful for our discussions here to sketch a Catholic view of the relations between religion and science. This may help also to begin the slow, somewhat painful, but crucial effort at forging a mutually comprehensible language for talking with one another, clearing away misunderstandings, and discerning those key facts that all of us will accept. This effort can only be begun. Yet, on its success, the usefulness of our converse depends. I will concentrate on the following points.

1. Catholic scientists hold that there is one God who created out of nothing this entire universe. Unlike the demiurges of nonbiblical religions, he needs no second principle of being that he is to shape or form or fashion. (Such a second principle, even perfectly formed, would remain intrinsically other than the goodness, intelligibility, and beauty that he would have impressed upon it. Hence, these religions tend ineluctably toward dualisms, with the material universe fundamentally opposed to the deity and to humanity—a poor soil for science). God is the one single principle of being for all that is; no evil principle exists.

2. The creature is, therefore, like God. Ultimately, there is nothing else for it to be like. Any other being it might be like is itself a creature, resembling God by every positive aspect of itself.

3. Yet, the creature is radically other than the Creator, who created in perfect freedom, without necessity, having no need of any creature.

---

[2]*Webster's New Collegiate Dictionary* (1956).

4. Being created by a God who is infinitely intelligent and wise, the universe is itself intelligible.

5. Since he is also infinite in goodness and in the power to effect perfectly what he desires so that the work fits his plan without defect, the entire creation is itself good, though limitedly so. It is, therefore, worthy to be known and understood to its least detail— as in Dr. Dyson's metaphor, to the least of the strange flora and fauna in that teeming jungle between the mountain peaks of an older physics.

6. Finally, because of that same infinite power, God's creatures too have power and are in continuous interaction with one another. Hence, no science can reduce to mere patterns or forms but must include actions and powers as integral to its explanations.

7. God also created intelligent beings, the pure spirits or angels and man. Man he created in his own image and likeness, hence intelligent, good, active, free, to be God's steward and cultivator of the universe. Both human beings and angels possess the power to understand the world and, in their own ways, act upon it for its good, developing its potentialities and their own.

8. Some angels sinned and led man to do the same. There resulted the disorders of disease and death, a dulling and levity of the mind, and a weakening of the will with a narrowing of the range of its freedom to choose.

9. This condition of sin, of ever-recurring moral evil, despite humanity's longing to do better, was met by God with the sending of a Redeemer, his own Son. He in whom, through whom, and for whom the universe was created became man; and the material world was united through his flesh, the same as ours, with its Creator as his Son. In this flesh, too, he died for our sins and rose that we might live a new life in him, by his power, not our own.

Hence, Christianity, from all aspects of its doctrine concerning God and concerning the fall and redemption, lies under an absolute and intrinsic necessity to affirm the goodness of the world, of our laboring to know and understand it, of our use of it, of our development of it. Science is, in consequence, a major means of serving God and praising him.

Those scientists, among whom Dr. Dyson numbers himself, who have but little knowledge of theology may find it helpful to know that Catholics distinguish rather sharply between matters of faith and matters of theology, despite the intimate connections between theology and faith. Of theologies (quite orthodox ones) there have been and still are a great number: those of St. Irenaeus, the Cappadocian Fathers, St. Augustine, St. Thomas Aquinas, Duns Scotus, St. Robert Bellarmine, Suarez, and many others down to our own day. But, in all their diversity and often mutual contradiction, they bear witness to one single teaching of faith.

The relationship between theologies and faith is rather like that of our sciences to the world about us. Faith involves a sharing by God of his own knowledge with us; the many theologies are human reflections in faith, both diverse and disciplined, upon what this divinely given mode of knowing opens to us. As the world is one, however various and contradictory our sciences, so, too, what we know through divine revelation is but one complex totality, however various and contradictory our theologies. (Perhaps it is well to point out that physics has always contained radically contradictory disciplines and that no genuine unity of physical science yet exists. Think only of the particle and field theories [based on an astronomical paradigm], thermodynamic theories [based on a chemical paradigm], and the continuing discussions concerning a radically probabilistic world versus an ultimately deterministic one.)

Heresy corresponds, then, not to the distortions that human understanding necessarily imposes on any projection of the faith but to falsifications. Though the most perfect of maps must involve some distortion, bad maps falsify, showing the continental United States contiguous with Hawaii and Alaska or putting only ocean between Mexico and Panama. In a similar way, heretical teaching denies some of the essential elements or aspects of what has been revealed or asserts as true things in contradiction to it.

Only in such a context can Catholic claims to divine truth be understood, whether accepted or not. Insofar as revelation is thought to give truth about mysteries otherwise wholly inaccessible to the human mind, this truth can be communicated only by the testimony of witnesses. Therefore, infallibility is not a matter of a "monopoly of truth," even in the domain of the understanding of the revelation, but of the accreditation and reliability of the witness. Catholics understand infallibility as a divine gift that makes it possible to transmit without falsification from generation to generation the essential contents of the revelation as first given.

Dr. Dyson sets a very high value on diversity and diversification. Yet, I would suggest that, in science no less than in religion, what matters most is neither unity nor diversity but their simultaneous coexistence. Mere diversification of species, intelligent or otherwise, should they lose the ability to communicate, should they cease to form part of an effectively single universe, would be of small interest. The grand vision of life spreading everywhere has emotional impact only for those who, in their mind's eye, can hold it all together.

So, too, the unicity of the Church need not be an obstacle to diversity. As one universe contains the endless variety of beings we know—and doubtless many more—so one Church is capable of containing all sorts of people. If the Church is truly a Body living with the life of the Spirit, then the more diversity the better, provided the unity of the whole Body and its good health is maintained. Just as for the diversity of theologies within the unity of faith, the limits to ecclesial diversity are set not by the need for unity, as such, but by the truth, the actual structures of reality.

As Dr. Dyson says, "Not everybody who worships God can or should be a Catholic." Indeed, the very possibility has been closed off for many. There are still vast regions of the world where most of the people have no chance whatsoever to hear anything of what Christians truly believe. And, of course, there were the countless centuries before the coming of Christ.

What H. G. Wells proposed as the common content of the great religions (and of much irreligion) represents a rather small portion of Catholic doctrine and ignores wholly the other aspects of our religion: the sacraments, the liturgy, the moral life, prayer, and, above all, the life in Christ. Though not unimportant, this common content is peripheral. It is, moreover, a good that cannot, in principle, be attained if once made into a goal.

Turning to Dr. Dyson's "five specific points at which faith and reason may appear to clash," I should like to say a few words about chance and randomness and then about the distinction between science and metascience. That done, more agreement with Dr. Dyson will seem possible than might appear from first glance.

Chance refers to those things that happen beyond our ability to foresee, even when we think we know their causes and their circumstances. The chance event in a deterministic universe occurs as the intersection of two causal chains that are—so far as our minds can see—wholly uncorrelated until this event takes place. In a world of randomly acting causes, *any* event will have some aspect of chance.

Randomness is a lack of causal sequence. Seemingly complete knowledge of the status of some prospective cause is insufficient for us to foresee which of several effects it may produce. We then speak of it as acting randomly. Whether our knowledge is truly adequate, or whether the process is truly random, is not here relevant.

Total randomness, if one can even conceive such a thing, can give rise to nothing at all. But, put in a few boundary conditions and a restriction, say, to dealing only with Markov processes and suddenly order appears—not from the randomness, as such, but from the order built into the process by the imposed constraints, along with the implicit order defining the random process of interest.

That randomness can exist at times only in the eye of the beholder has been shown by mathematicians in a particularly simple fashion. You all know that the ratio of the circumference of a circle to its diameter is pi = 3.14159265358979323846. . . . Nothing can be more completely specified and determinate, and the calculation of the further decimal places has been carried out far beyond any practical use one might have—save one. If you take this figure not as the representation of a single number but as a sequence of digits, the sequence has all the properties mathematicians have been able to specify that would enable them to detect a purely random sequence.

The difficulty concerning the origin of life, the first of Dr. Dyson's five points, gets its bite from considering chance in the processes of the physical universe to be in some sort of competition with the certainty of God's plan. Thence, to accept God's certain knowledge of all outcomes would be to deny the existence of genuinely chance events, a denial that quantum theory would seem to rule out.

But, in fact, the agent, all its potentialities, and its random actualizing of them are in their totality held in being by God. He knows things not by inference from causes but by being the Cause that makes all causes to be and that determines whether they are to act randomly on the created order and how.

Catholic faith, for all its insistence that God is both omniscient and omnipotent, has always held, against all comers, the freedom of the human will. This freedom is hard to understand, even when considered without reference to God, for there is nothing in our experience that is similar to it or that is more "given" or, yet, simpler. In fact, as we might expect *a priori*, it is the existence of "an omniscient and omnipotent God" that, far from exacerbating the problem, offers a clue to its solution. For, if God is free, then one created according to his image and in his likeness must share in such an essential perfection.

Human freedom is not a phenomenon of randomness as Planck seems to have thought. Surely, we have all experienced in times of illness or abstractedness the entertaining of random thoughts, the doing of random acts. We are acutely conscious that in each case we have not, for the nonce, been acting freely. The constraints on our thoughts or actions are not, then, external to us; but, we are aware of them, however hidden in themselves, as determining our actions.

There is no time to develop the matter here; but, just as we cannot act freely without knowledge of the options, so we cannot know that one thing is true or another false unless we can supplement the indeterminacy of our mental powers by a free decision to accept this evidence or to reject that. Knowledge of truth and freedom of the will are correlative, neither involving randomness of any sort.

When we turn to "the problem of forbidden teleology" and the relations between science and metascience, we may find it helpful to range more broadly and look at the differences between science and whatever is manifestly not science, for example, history, art, and literature. For, even without going to the abstractness of philosophy, we should note that there are many ways we can ask reasonable questions and obtain reasonable answers without doing science.

Physical science is, by definition, restricted not simply to the material but to what can be somehow dealt with in quantitative terms, with what is somehow sensibly measurable and publicly verifiable. Or, as I should prefer to put it, physical science deals with the search for isomorphisms between the structures and processes of our world and the various pure forms of mathematics. All else is, in principle, excluded from its concern and its competence.[3]

Hence, science has no standing even to ask, much less answer, the sort of teleological questions Dr. Dyson has raised. Scientists can indeed argue for or against purposefulness, but only because they are human beings first and scientists by specialization. Dr. Dyson's solution, then, is quite acceptable—or so it seems to me—whatever one may think of the anthropic principle. Purpose is one

---

[3]The "all else" here refers to the object of science, what it seeks or claims to know, not to the process of doing science itself, which modern philosophers have delighted to show is highly nonquantifiable psychosocial activity.

of the topics that science, by its own choice of method, simply does not have the tools to deal with.

The question about the argument from design must be resolved in similar fashion. This argument has always been and should remain the professional property of the philosopher. Dr. Dyson, however, has framed it in an interesting way, transforming it into a problem that has much exercised the British analysts in years past. How can one recognize the other persons? By what criteria can one be sure that one is dealing with another mind?

This problem has, I think, no solution as it is usually intended. For, what is sought is some sort of fully objective, publicly verifiable, universally applicable, and impersonal set of criteria that can be applied to putative persons to determine whether they are truly such or not. But, precisely as persons, they are not capable of being impersonally demonstrated or proved or experimentally tested for. Again, science has no standing to ask about them. So, again, I should agree with Dr. Dyson that one must go to metascience for both the question and its possible answers.

Many currents in contemporary philosophy would argue that we recognize other people through processes akin to those by which we learn something about the author of a book by reading his work or about one who speaks with us by responding to him in human fashion. That we could be fooled by a sufficiently cleverly designed automaton would only be to mistake the location of the sufficiently clever mind that did the designing.

As to Dr. Dyson's fifth and final question, I confess to having little concern for the grand expansion of life all over this galaxy and others. Yet, I find it of interest theologically that physics plus imagination can come up with a new response to the old question: What divine purpose might there be for having left such vast spaces uninhabited?—if indeed they are.

I should find adequate as a purpose for such immensities their use to manifest the greater immensity of the human mind. Seated on this speck of the Earth, the mind can reach out and weigh the galaxies and find the laws governing the evolution, not merely of amoebae and dinosaurs but of stars and universes.

I agree with Dr. Dyson that reading the mind of God is a somewhat venturesome and not usually successful task. Fortunately, having solved the problem of other persons by creating us, God has gone further and spoken to us, to tell us his mind and reveal to us why he made us and why there is so much suffering.

Dr. Dyson's principle of maximum diversity is not without its possible basis in Scripture, and the Christian's answer to his question does speak of a life for which this one prepares us, as a caterpillar's does for its metamorphosis. But note: the butterfly "flies defenseless to the Judgment Throne." There is an ultimate tragedy as well as an ultimate triumph. This ultimate diversity is indeed maximum; no greater one can be conceived.

The purpose of at least part of what God has done is to lead as many of us as he can, individually and together, to the triumph. Then, we do not remain in Purgatory but, by his mercy, fly up until we see, united in their Source, the scattered leaves of the book of nature, which we, as scientists, tried so hard to read. Further yet, we see as it were three rainbows, each reflecting in full the others, and gaze upon the Love that moves the sun and the other stars (*Paradiso*, Canto 33).

Discussion

BISHOP EGAN: Three discussion groups have volunteered to share their reflections on Dr. Dyson's and Fr. Quay's comments.

DR. ALICE B. HAYES: Our table spent some time discussing the problem of the omniscience of God and human free will. Dr. Lejeune offered a helpful analogy that reminded us of the limitations of our own minds. Just as physicists accept wave-particle duality, comfortably assuming it in predictions of experimental results, so we can, in faith, accept the duality of free will and God's omniscience. In both cases, the dichotomies must be seen as complementary: the omniscience of God and free will can be accepted together as mutually exclusive facets of reality. The existence of the particle-wave duality does not impede the development of physics. In the same way, the free will-omniscience duality need not disturb faith.

We also discussed the nature of law in science and theology. Law in science is represented by calculational schemes that predict the outcome of natural and experimental events. We remain open to changing these laws as new observations and insights require; in science, the final laws are never written. There seems to be less openness to change in religion, though we recognize that doctrine develops over time and that there is always a range of theological opinion. Certainly, a defined doctrine is less readily changed than a scientific law.

FR. ROBERT BRUNGS, SJ: During the Wilberforce-Huxley confrontation on evolution, *Punch* ran a cartoon depicting a primate in a cage in the London Zoo. The caption was "Am I my keeper's brother?" In a way, that sums up the rather tangled relation between science and religion.

When one says "orthodoxy," one thinks of religion. But, there is also an element of orthodoxy in science. These orthodoxies may include method, central ideas, or both; a certain amount of ortho-doxy is necessary to science.

On the other hand, all search for truth, whether it be religious or scientific truth, involves trial and error. The scientific publications usually don't mention the ninety-nine false solutions the experimenter pursued before finding the true one. They don't mention the cul-de-sacs to which so much scientific research leads. In the same way, many major religious doctrines came to definition through controversy. Thus, while there are givens in both religion and science, a fuller understanding emerges only from trial and error and controversy. There will always be more to know, both for the scientist and the religionist. It will take us literally forever to work out our understanding of God-made-man, and of the creation we live in.

FR. JOSEPH BRACKEN, SJ: My group talked at length about the character of truth in science and religion. We agree that science pursues its equivalent of absolute truth. But, should it be understood in the same way as absolute truth in religion, particularly as regards infallible declarations? Certainly, there are things that scientists take for granted, but are they held with the same finality as religious doctrines? Are there differences between the definitions of "true statement" as used in science and in religion? In the same way, while authority plays a role in science as in religion, are there differences in the use of authority in the two fields?

We also wrestled with the question of God's omniscience. Is he ignorant, in some measure, of what is going to happen? Most of us thought: "No. God knows everything in his eternality. Past, present, and future have no significance for him." Others, however, objected: "If something isn't real yet, if it isn't actual yet, can even God know it as real? In other words, can the future be present to God?"

We reviewed Fr. Quay's understanding of chance as intersecting lines of causality, and the issue of spontaneity arose. In principle, intersecting lines of causality can be known by an omniscient mind. But, consider spontaneity in the strict sense. Can a truly spontaneous event be known in advance, even by an infinite mind, without negating its spontaneity? If so, God knows created potentiality perfectly, not just its possibilities, but all its actualizations. The question inevitably arises: Is that deterministic by implication or not? Some say: "No. God could know a created potentiality as

being inherently free and, therefore, would know it in its freedom."
The point, obviously, is open to debate.

A final reflection. Dr. Dyson quoted H. G. Wells's description
of the human person as "a being at first scattered and blind and
utterly confused, feeling its way slowly to the serenity and salvation
of an ordered and coherent purpose." If one believes that the
universe embodies its own growth and purpose, would one feel any
need or desire to accept a personal God? Even more to the point,
from a Christian perspective, does such a formulation leave any
room for an Incarnation and Redemption?

BISHOP EGAN: Perhaps, we should ask Dr. Dyson and Fr. Quay
if they have any reactions to these comments.

DR. DYSON: While I haven't had time to sort it out, one point
deserves mention. The relative place of age and youth in the cultures of science and religion seems very important. I, as a scientist,
am in the happy situation where nobody needs to take me seriously
anymore. Science is dominated by younger people. We veterans
are constantly being pushed aside and put on the shelf. In organized
religion, on the other hand, the elders, the bishops, really do count
for something. There is a much larger hierarchical element in religion, and that is a cause of difficulty. This should be noted.

FR. MCMULLIN: I hoped that Dr. Dyson would speak about the
anthropic principle. His book *Disturbing the Universe* contains a chapter called "The Argument from Design." That chapter has given
rise to very lively controversy; Stephen Jay Gould and others have
addressed it.

Let me briefly outline the anthropic principle. At the beginning
of the seventeenth century, Descartes suggested that if the universe
begins from a random chaos of particles in random motion, these
particles will aggregate into stars and planets. Ultimately, following
simply the laws of nature, life will originate and become intelligent.
In other words, an initial state of chaos will gravitate toward com-
plexification and toward life.

In the 1920s, the development of general relativity theory and
the discovery of the expansion of the universe permitted the formulation of a cosmology. For the first time since the Greek period,
a cosmology became possible because there was now a theory that
could encompass the universe. Although Newton's infinite space
is not comprehensible, Einstein's new space is. You can roughly
calculate the number of particles in the universe, its radius, its
volume.

But, when this cosmology was formulated, when the physicists applied quantum mechanics to the first microseconds of the universe, they discovered that the development of a life-bearing universe is almost infinitely improbable. An initial state suitable for the development of life is a very odd state indeed; Stephen Hawking has said that technically it has a probability of zero. Nevertheless, here we are! The universe has, in fact, produced life. The assertion that the presence of life in the universe in some way serves to explain the existence of the universe itself is called the anthropic principle.

Inquiries about early stages of the universe seem to fall within the realm of physics. But the anthropic principle raises a question that physics is incapable of answering because it is an existential question: Why should our universe exist instead of some other universe that lacks the conditions necessary for the development of life?

DR. JOAN ROBERTS: In Hawking's work, is it life that is improbable or matter?

FR. MCMULLIN: Matter raises no difficulties, because "matter," as Dr. Dyson has said, is a very loose term for many different states. The initial state of the universe was, of course, in some broad sense matter.

DR. ROBERTS: No, that is where we disagree. The grand unification theories start with a force before there was matter, then move to energy and then to the formation of matter. The improbability lies at this point. Both matter and antimatter existed at the early stages. They annihilate one another. Hawking says there is zero probability that the universe contained only a bit more matter than antimatter, and that the matter now in existence is the "overage," so to speak. From a chemist's point of view, making life was easy once matter was there. Making matter was the hard trick.

FR. MCMULLIN: We don't really have the language to discuss the extremely early stages of the universe when extraordinarily high energies ruled. I would prefer to use the philosopher's term "matter" all the way back to the beginning, even for the energy states that preceded the formation of matter in the form of particles. That is a matter of choice. You are correct in saying that the balance between antimatter and matter is one of the important factors. It is not the only one by any means, however.

The issue is this. Life seems to lay quite a number of constraints on the kind of universe it will inhabit. You need, for example, a universe that is not purely hydrogen and helium; the heavier elements must have evolved. You also need a relatively long-lived universe so that evolution can occur. There are perhaps twenty or thirty different constraints that apply.

SR. LAURA LANDEN, OP: Dr. Dyson, I have a question on a matter that seems to be fundamental to your view of science. Near the beginning of your talk, you mentioned that science is the free creation of the human mind. Somewhat later, you said that the domains of science and religion can exist comfortably within the same individual provided each is granted its autonomy. You believe, if I understand you correctly, that science does not consider any statement "infallible"; every scientific assertion is ultimately open to revision. Is this indeed your position? Is there absolutely nothing that the scientist considers beyond debate, for example, the existence of electrons? Does science ever attain knowledge that can be held with certitude?

DR. DYSON: The answer is, of course, "yes." We scientists are not being consistent when we claim that all statements are open to doubt. In daily life, we take a great many things for granted not only the existence of electrons but, more important, the discipline of the field in which we happen to be working, which is a public discipline and which defines whether one is a scientist or not. The discipline is quite authoritarian. If one doesn't follow the rules of the game, he will be disregarded or considered a crackpot. We scientists cut mavericks out in a very merciless fashion. We don't practice what we preach any more than other people do.

In principle, on the other hand, even the existence of electrons *is* open to question. If someone came along with a new way of looking at things in which electrons were irrelevant, no doubt we would all climb on that bandwagon. But, we are not as free in our daily utterances as we would like to pretend. Discipline is a very important part of science, just as freedom is. The two must be held in balance. The discipline can be quite rigid, and many people have felt the lash.

SR. LANDEN: I find it curious that you seem to split science and religion into two radically distinct domains and, yet, discuss something like the argument from design. What is it that you think the argument from design shows? If this argument belongs to science, even in the sense of metascience, is it not a common ground subject both to religious and scientific investigation?

DR. DYSON: The fact that religion and science are distinct domains doesn't mean that they do not overlap. There are quite wide ranges of thought and discourse where both are relevant.

SR. LANDEN: But, you maintain that they are radically distinct domains that should maintain their autonomy?

DR. DYSON: Yes. But, that doesn't mean that religion and science cannot talk to each other or argue with each other or even come into dispute. Disputes in themselves are not evil; it is only when they become legalistic that they do harm.

DR. LAWRENCE ULRICH: Our group discussed the problem and possibility of ongoing dialogue at some length. Dr. Dyson takes a view of science grounded upon the development of *a posteriori* knowledge and the acknowledgement of diversity. This, in turn, gives rise to the possibility of unlimited discussion. Even though we may presently accept the existence of electrons, dialogue on the point remains an option. On the other hand, I think Fr. Quay took an *a priori* stance.

One of my concerns as a philosopher is that *a priori* stances lead to orthodoxy, shutting down discussion. When you accept a statement that is not open to testing, the sort of dialogue that allows people to talk about things as though they really matter cannot occur. Once one takes an *a priori* position, it is easy to dismiss other people as irrelevant or, at most, "interesting." This is a central consideration as scientists and religious leaders sit down to talk.

FR. QUAY: *A posteriori* is the Latin for "arguing from something behind you," while *a priori* is "arguing from something in front." Both imply a reference point. I would respond, then, that all of us, whatever we say, argue from our past experience, our convictions, the things we take as true on whatever grounds. There is no other way of entering into discussion, even with ourselves. In that limited sense, everyone speaks *a posteriori*.

On the other hand, once certain points are reasonably well nailed down, they become harder and harder to debate without going back to the fundamentals on which they are based. So, while we could discuss with an enormous amount of richness and diversity the positions I have taken with regard to creation, revelation, the communicability of revelation, and the rest, these things would have to be treated in a much broader context than can be adopted here. In any discussion, it is essential to recognize the ambit within which we can talk more or less intelligently, limiting ourselves to an occasional foray outside to define a term more carefully or to clarify something.

DR. ULRICH: That is a very helpful elucidation. Knowledge of our starting point is central to entering into useful dialogue. We must communicate our experience which, if we are a diverse group, is going to be very diverse. While some may have greater confidence in their experience, that greater confidence does not give their position any special privilege. Archbishop Hickey invited us last evening to begin an open and free dialogue, communicating our experiences of the world and our belief systems so we can eventually see where commonality exists. Even commonality, however, doesn't mean certitude. That is what science teaches us. While scientists can come to a general, tentative consensus, that consensus is always testable. We must remain open.

FR. BENEDICT ASHLEY, OP: Dr. Dyson gave us a very attractive answer to the basic question we are asking, namely, Is there some way to bring a religious view and a scientific view into fruitful relation to each other? He gave us a picture of science that is essentially a religious interpretation, but one consistent with present scientific knowledge.

As attractive as this model is, especially to theologians who accept the philosophy of Whitehead as a proper understanding of the universe, it does raise a serious problem for Catholic orthodoxy. I grant that the universe shows a kind of mind that penetrates all things and confers order on reality. It has produced humanity; above all, it has produced scientists, who are able to understand the universe and to exercise a certain control over it. Mind penetrates the whole of this.

As Fr. McMullin has shown us, the biblical view is that the Jewish God is utterly independent of the universe. In Dyson's model, on the other hand, God as mind is somehow part of the universe. So, we have a contrast between two models: one that posits a mind-filled universe and another that posits God, the eternal spirit, and a temporal universe molded and formed by God and therefore exhibiting the characteristics of mind. I would ask Dr. Dyson why he prefers his model to the biblical one. They have much in common and agree on the existence of an orderly universe. If Dr. Dyson could choose the biblical model with a transcendent God, I for one would have less difficulty in finding common ground with him.

DR. DYSON: I would have to go into my whole personal history in order properly to answer that question, which would be inappropriate here. I grew up in a very grim time. I was brought up as a Christian. But, I looked at the world in the 1930s with the powers of evil gathering and the world apparently going rapidly to hell. It just didn't look like anything a transcendent God would have wanted to have anything to do with. I suppose that is the crucible in which my religious views were formed. Those years were so grim as to shake one's faith in anything, certainly to shake one's faith in a transcendent God.

RELIGION AND EVOLUTIONARY THEORY

PRESIDER
Most Rev. Howard J. Hubbard
Bishop of Albany

SPEAKER
Dr. Edward O. Wilson
Frank B. Baird, Jr., Professor of Science
Harvard University

RESPONDENT
Rev. Thomas M. King, SJ
Associate Professor of Theology
Georgetown University

DISCUSSION

Dr. Edward O. Wilson

At the Cologne Cathedral, in 1980, Pope John Paul II said that science has added "wings to the spirit of modern awareness." Yet, science does not threaten the core of religious belief: "We have no fear, indeed we regard it as excluded, that a branch of science or branch of knowledge, based on reason and proceeding methodically and securely, can arrive at knowledge that comes into conflict with the truth of faith. This can be the case only where the differentiation between the orders of knowledge is overlooked or denied."

That last sentence, reaffirming Augustine's two books of God, takes us to the heart of the real dialogue between religion and science. Although many theologians and lay philosophers like to deny it, I believe that traditional religious belief and scientific knowledge depict the universe in radically different ways. At bedrock, they are incompatible and mutually exclusive. The materialist (or "humanist" or "naturalist") position can be put in a phrase: there is only one book, and it was written in a manner too strange and subtle to be foretold by the prophets and church fathers.

But, there is another side to the story, one that makes the contrast in world views still more interesting. The materialist position presupposes no final answers. It is an undeniable fact that faith is in our bones, that religious belief is a part of human nature and seemingly vital to social existence. Take away one faith, and another rushes in to fill the void. Take away that, and some secular equivalent such as Marxism intrudes, replete with sacred texts and icons. Take away all these faiths and rely wholly on skepticism and personal inquiry—if you can—and the fabric of society would likely start to unravel. This phenomenon, so strange and subtle as to daunt materialist explanation, is in my opinion the most promising focus for a dialogue between theologians and scientists.

From early Greek philosophy, there has always been a great divide in thought. Humanity is faced with a choice between two metaphysics, two differing views of how the world works from the top down and, hence, of the ultimate means for the selection of moral codes. The first view holds that morality is transcendental in origin and exists both within and apart from the human species. This doctrine has been refined within the Church by the conception of natural law, which is the reading of the eternal law in God's mind: People reason out God's intent through a reflection of human nature, obedient to the principle that, as Aquinas expressed it, "man has a natural inclination to know the truth about God and to live in society." The opposing view is that morality is entirely a human phenomenon. In the modern, evolutionary version of this materialist philosophy, its precepts represent the upwelling of deep impulses that are encoded in our genes and find expression within the setting of particular cultures. They have nothing directly to do with divine guidance, at least not in the manner conceived by traditional religions.

I may be wrong (and, in any case, do not speak for all scientists), but I believe that the correct metaphysic is the materialist one. It works in the following way. Our profound impulses are rooted in a genetic heritage common to the entire species. They arose by evolution through natural selection over a period of tens or hundreds of thousands of years. These propensities provide survival for individuals and for the social groups on which personal survival depends. They are transmuted through rational process and the formation of culture into specific moral codes that are integrated into religion and the sacralized memories of revolutions, conquests, and other historical events by which cultures secured their survival. Although variations in the final codes are inevitable, different societies share a great deal in their perception of right and wrong. By making the search for these similarities part of the scientific enterprise, and by taking religious behavior very seriously as a key part of genetically evolved human nature, a tighter consensus on ethical behavior might be reached.

Let me interpose, at this point, a very brief account of evolution by natural selection. Genetic variation among individuals in a population of the same species, say a population of human beings, arises by mutations, which are random changes in the chemical composition and relative positions of genes. Of the thousands of mutations that typically occur throughout a population in each generation, all but a minute fraction are either neutral in effect or deleterious to some degree. They include, for example, the altered genes that cause hemophilia and Tay-Sachs disease and the abnormally duplicated chromosomes responsible for Down's syndrome. When a new mutant (or novel combination of rare preexisting genes) happens to be superior to the ordinary "normal" genes, it tends to spread through the population over a period of many generations and, hence, become by definition the new genetic norm. If human beings were to move into a new environment that somehow gave hemophiliacs a survival and reproductive advantage over nonhemophiliacs, then, in time, hemophilia would predominate in the population and be regarded as the norm.

Two features of evolution by natural selection conspire to give it extraordinary creative potential. The first is the driving power of mutations. All populations are subject to a continuous rain of new genetic types that test the old. The second feature is the ability of natural selection to create immensely complicated new structures and physiological processes, including new patterns of behavior, with no blueprint and no force behind them other than the selection process itself. This is a key point missed by creationists and other critics of evolutionary theory, who often argue that the probability of assembling an eye or a hand (or life itself) by genetic mutations is infinitesimally small—in effect, impossible. But, the following thought experiment shows that the opposite is true. Suppose that a new trait emerges if two new gene forms (mutations), which I will call A and B, occur simultaneously. The chances of A occurring are one in a million, and the chances of B occurring are also one in a million. Then, the chances of both A and B occurring simultaneously as mutants are one in a trillion, a near impossibility—as the critics intuited. However, natural selection subverts this process. If A has even a slight advantage by itself alone, it will become the dominant gene at its position. Now, the chances of AB appearing are one in a million. In even moderately sized species of plants and animals (which often contain more than a million individuals), the changeover to AB is a virtual certainty.

This very simple picture of evolution at the level of the gene has altered our conception of both the nature of life and humanity's place in nature. Before Darwin, it was customary to use the great complexity of living organisms per se as proof of the existence of God. The most famous expositor of this "argument from design" was the Reverend William Paley, who in 1802 introduced the watchmaker analogy: the existence of a watch implies the existence of a watchmaker. In other words, great effects imply great causes. Common sense would seem to dictate the truth of this deduction, but common sense, as Einstein once noted, is only our accumulated experience up to the age of eighteen. Common sense tells us that one-ton satellites cannot hang suspended 200 miles above a point on the earth's surface, but they do.

We have arrived at the conception of the one book of creation to which I alluded earlier. Given the combination of mutation and natural selection, the biological equivalent of watches can be created without a watchmaker. But, did blind natural selection also lead to the human mind, including moral behavior and spirituality? That is the grandmother of questions in both biology and the humanities. Common sense would seem, at first, to dictate the answer to be "No." But, I and many other scientists believe that the answer may be "Yes." Furthermore, it is possible by this means to explain the very meaning of human life.

The key proposition based on evolutionary biology is the following: Everything human, including the mind and culture, has a material basis and originated during the evolution of the human genetic constitution and its interaction with the environment. To say this much is not to deny the great creative power of culture or to minimize the fact that most causes of human thought and behavior are still poorly understood. The important point is that modern biology already can account for many of the unique properties of our species. Research on that subject is accelerating quickly enough to lend plausibility to the proposition that more complex forms of social behavior, including religious belief and moral reasoning, will eventually be understood to their foundations.

A case in point, useful for its simplicity and tractability, is the avoidance of brother-sister incest. In order to avoid misunderstanding, let me define *incest* as strong sexual bonding among close biological relatives that includes intercourse of the kind generally associated with cohabitation and procreation and excludes transient forms of adolescent experimentation. Incest taboos are very nearly universal and a cultural norm. The avoidance of brother-sister incest originates in what psychologists have called prepared learning. This means that people are innately prone to learn one alternative as opposed to another. They pick it up more readily, they enjoy it more, or both. The avoidance of sibling incest comes from the "potty rule" in mental development: individuals reared in close domestic proximity during the first six years of life (they share the same potty) are automatically inhibited from strong sexual attraction and bonding when they reach sexual maturity. The rule works even when the children reared together are biologically unrelated and later encouraged to marry and have children, as in the Israeli *kib-butzim* and traditional minor marriages of prerevolutionary China. Those affected are usually quite unable to offer a rational explanation of why they have no attraction. Some unconscious process ticked over in the brain and the urge, they explain, never came.

The inhibitory rule is an example not only of prepared learning but also of "proximate causation" as it is understood by evolutionary biologists. This means that the learning channels a response of importance to the survival or reproduction of the organism. Proximate causes are put into place by the assembly of genes through the process of natural selection. The ultimate causation—in other words, the particular selection regime that enabled certain genes to predominate in the first place—is the well-documented effect of inbreeding depression. When mating occurs between brother and sister, father and daughter, or mother and son, the probability of matching debilitating genes in both homologous chromosomes of the offspring is greatly increased. The end result is a rise in abortion, physical defects, and genetic disease. Hence, genes prescribing a biological propensity to avoid incest will be favored over those that do not. Most animal and plant species display proximate devices of one kind or another, and it does indeed protect them from inbreeding depression. In some, the response is rigidly determined. In others, especially the brighter mammals, it is based on prepared learning. Interestingly enough, the human proximate form is nearly identical to that of the chimpanzee, the species to which we are most closely related genetically.

It is exquisitely human to semanticize innate tendencies. In many societies, incest avoidance is underwritten by symbolically transmitted taboos, myths, and laws. These, not the emotions and programs of prepared learning, are the values we perceive by direct, casual observation. They are easily transmitted from one person to the next, and they are the behaviors most readily studied by scholars. But, the phenomenon of greatest interest is the etiology of the moral behavior: the chain of events leading from ultimate cause in natural selection to proximate cause in prepared learning to reification and legitimation in culture. If the terminal cultural form were somehow to be stripped away by a collective loss of memory, people would still avoid sibling incest. Given enough time, they would most likely invent religious and ethical rationalizations to justify their feelings about the wrongness of incest.

Crude genetic determinism has no part in this process. The existence of the three-step etiology in mental development, genes to learning rules to culture, in no way contradicts free will. Individual choice persists, even when learning is strongly prepared by heredity. If some future society decides to encourage brother-sister incest, for whatever bizarre and unlikely reason, it now has the knowledge to do so efficiently. The possibility, however, is vanishingly remote, because the same knowledge tells us that incest avoidance is programmed as a powerful rule and protects families from genetic damage. We are likely to agree still more firmly than before that the avoidance is a part of human nature to be fostered. In short, incest avoidance is and will continue to be one of our common values.

It will immediately occur to you that incest avoidance might be no more than a special case in the evolution of social behavior. A vast difference separates this relatively simple phenomenon from economic cycles, religious rites, and presidential elections. Might such particularities fall within a wholly different domain of explanation and require a different metaethic? Perhaps, but I don't think so.

The evidence favoring the evolutionary approach to moral reasoning is as follows. By mid-1985, no fewer than 3,577 human genes had been identified, of which about 600 had been placed on one or another of the 23 pairs of chromosomes. This is a respectable fraction of the entire human complement. New techniques for separation and identification make it possible to map most of the genes and specify all of the DNA sequences—perhaps, by early in the next century. Hundreds of the genes already known alter behavior in one way or another. In most cases, the effect is crude or indirect. But, a few change behavior in a precise manner as, for example, those modulating depression, reading ability, and performance on spatial tests. Twins and adoption studies have implicated other genes—as yet unmapped and probably working in complex multiples—in schizophrenia, propensity toward homosexuality, performance on tests measuring empathy, and a wide range of personality traits from introversion/extroversion to athleticism and proneness to alcoholism. Moreover, prepared learning and biases in perception have been discovered in virtually every category of behavior thus far studied. In their seminal book *The Biology of Religion*, Vernon Reynolds and Ralph Tanner showed that

survival and genetic reproduction can be favored by the traditional
practices of religion, including evangelism, marriage rites, and even
celibacy and asceticism, the latter through their positive effects on
group cohesion and welfare.

But, to come quickly to the point that most troubles critics of
evolutionary ethics, it does not follow that the genetic programs of
cognition and prepared learning are automatically beneficial, even
in a crude Darwinian sense. Behaviors such as xenophobia and
territorial expansion may have been very adaptive in the earlier,
formative stages of human evolutionary history, but they are destructive now, even for those who practice them. Although the
cultural *ought* is more tightly linked to the genetic *is* than philosophers have traditionally conceded, the two do not automatically
translate one into the other. A workable moral code can be obtained
not just by understanding the foundations of human nature but by
the wise choice of those constraints needed to keep us alive and
free in a rapidly changing cultural environment that renders some
of our propensities maladaptive.

Let me illustrate this approach to moral reasoning by taking an
example that has proved troublesome to the Church. In *Humanae
Vitae*, Pope Paul VI used the best interpretation concerning human
nature available to him to proscribe artificial birth control and to
protect the family. He said, in effect, that you should not prevent
conception when having sex because that is what sex is for and, as
such, reflects the will of God: "To use this divine gift destroying,
even if only partially, its meaning and its purpose is to contradict
the nature both of man and of woman and of their most intimate
relationship, and, therefore, it is to contradict also the plan of God
and his will."

I believe that there is a way out of the impasse that this strict
argument from natural law has created. All that we have learned
of biology in recent years suggests that the perception of human
nature expressed by Pope Paul VI was only half true. A second
major function of sexual intercourse, one evolved over vast periods
of time, is the bonding of couples in a manner that enhances the
long-term care of children. Only a minute fraction of sexual acts
can result in conception, but virtually all can tighten the conjugal
bonds. Many circumstances can be imagined, and in fact exist, in
which family planning by artificial birth control leads to an improvement of the bonding function while promoting the rearing of
healthy, secure children.

If this more recent and better substantiated view of human sexuality is accepted, a revision of *Humanae Vitae* could easily be written that accomplishes the main purpose of Pope Paul VI and the modern Church, permits artificial birth control, and, in fact, serves as a model of the utilization of scientific findings by religious thinkers.

I am now going to close with a truly radical suggestion: The choice among the foundation of moral reasoning is not likely to remain arbitrary. Metaethics can be tested empirically. One system of ethics and, hence, one kind of religion is not as good as another. Not only are some less workable, they are, in the profoundest sense, less human. The corollary is that people can be educated readily only to a narrow range of ethical precepts. This leaves a choice between evolutionary ethics and transcendentalism. The idea of a genetic origin of moral codes can be further tested by a continuance of biological studies of complex human behavior, including religious thought itself. To the extent that the sensory and nervous systems appear to have evolved by natural selection or some other purely natural process, the evolutionary interpretation will be supported. To the extent that they do not appear to have evolved in this manner, or to the extent that complex human behavior cannot be linked to a physical basis in the sensory and nervous systems, the evolutionary explanation will have to be abandoned and a transcendental explanation sought.

Which position—scientific materialism or religious transcendentalism—proves correct will eventually make a very great difference in how humanity views itself and plans its future. But, for the years immediately ahead, this distinction makes little difference if the following overriding fact is realized: Human nature is, at the very least, far more a product of self-contained evolution than ordinarily conceded by philosophers and theologians. On the other hand, religious thought is far richer and more subtle than present-day science can explain—and too important to abandon. Meanwhile, the areas of common concern are vast, and the two enterprises can converge in most of the areas of practical moral reasoning at the same time that their practitioners disagree about the ultimate causes of human nature.

What, then, is the best relation between religion and science toward which we might aim? I would say an uneasy but fruitful alliance. The role of religion is to codify and put into enduring poetic form the highest moral values of a society consistent with empirical knowledge and to lead in moral reasoning. The role of science is to test remorselessly every conclusion about human nature and to search for the bedrock of ethics—by which I mean the material basis of natural law. Science faces in religion its most interesting challenge, while religion will find in science the necessary means to meet the modern age.

Rev. Thomas M. King, SJ

I speak as a theologian-philosopher, not as a biologist. Yet, because of an interest in the theology-evolution debate, I long have been aware of the impressive research of Dr. Wilson. As one sympathetic to the thought of Teilhard de Chardin, I have followed with interest Dr. Wilson's integration of social structures into biology. Again with Teilhard, Dr. Wilson has stressed the motivational importance of religion in human survival.

In today's world, many noted evolutionists have made religious hostility integral to their literary style. It is a legacy from Thomas Huxley and Ernst Haeckel in the last century and has been aggravated by court battles in this century. Most of us are familiar with the style from hearing Carl Sagan on television, but it is also found in Jacques Monod, Francois Jacob, Francis Crick, Richard Dawkins, and numerous others. Thus, I have appreciated the gracious presentation we have just heard and its call for a "fruitful alliance" between religion and science, especially since Dr. Wilson is widely known for challenging the whole substance of religion. I will touch on this, but I am here to respond to the paper we have just heard; in doing so, I will tell of two ambiguities and two difficulties.

The first ambiguity: Dr. Wilson's paper uses St. Augustine's image of two books: the Bible and the natural world. Dr. Wilson would limit himself to the natural world. For Augustine, the natural world spoke of God as much as did the Bible. While we are not here to discuss the texts of Augustine, in calling himself a materialist and endorsing a materialist metaphysic, Dr. Wilson *seems* to be using a condensed version of Augustine's book of nature. Or is he? That is my first ambiguity.

Let me explain. Dr. Wilson speaks of people being called upon to make free choices, yet many materialists would claim there are no free choices. More important, he has just spoken of moral precepts that "have nothing directly to do with divine guidance, at least not in the manner conceived by traditional religion." A striking sentence that suggests an *indirect* divine guidance and a new way of conceiving of it! Elsewhere, Dr. Wilson has said, "Deity can still be sought in the origin of the ultimate units of matter, in quarks and electron shells. . . ."[1] and "God remains a viable hypothesis as the prime mover."[2] He is unwilling to call himself an agnostic, as he is not averse to the idea of some intelligence or force that gave the universe its initial form. Thus, the "materialist" metaphysics of Dr. Wilson includes free choice, an ethic, and a natural theology according to which God planned and indirectly guides the universe! I do not see how it remains a materialist metaphysics.

My second ambiguity: Today, Dr. Wilson has spoken of a dialogue between theologians and scientists and a fruitful alliance between religion and science. An intellectual dialogue implies that each side has a partial grasp of the truth, yet I am not sure Dr. Wilson would allow this to the theologian. He claims that "traditional religious belief and scientific knowledge . . . at bedrock . . . are incompatible and mutually exclusive." Yet, this exclusivity will not make a difference in "the years immediately ahead." He also speaks of religious thought having something "more subtle than *present-day* science can explain."

I would read these statements as implying that future science will explain religion, which can then be dispensed with. Theologians—not bishops—will be the first to go. This is Dr. Wilson's general position. He claims that religion will erode away when people recognize religious beliefs are "really enabling mechanisms for survival"—something that theologians will be the first to admit! I would respond to this charge in terms of a book titled *Just Because I Have Paranoia Does Not Mean that I Am Not Being Persecuted*. Just because religion enables people to survive does not mean that its content is illusion. The eyes could also be called "enabling mechanisms for survival," but this does not mean that what they see is not really there. So with the religious sense; it, too, can be an opening to truth.

In his call for a fruitful alliance between science and religion, Edward Wilson has assigned religion the role of giving "enduring and poetic form" to the highest moral values of society. Being aware of the general context of his thought, it would seem he is asking religion to add emotional fuzz to values developed elsewhere. As a theologian, I want a larger share of the pie.

---

[1]Edward O. Wilson, *On Human Nature* (Cambridge, Mass.: Harvard University Press, 1978), p. 1.

[2]Ibid., p. 191.

The third point: In calling for a materialist metaphysics, Dr. Wilson also wants an ethics. He speaks of ways of keeping us "alive and free." Life and freedom are here presented as values; but, how can values come from materialist metaphysics? One configuration of matter is or is not as good as another. Dr. Wilson even tells of a metaethics that "can be tested empirically." I would claim that a materialist metaphysics will not provide values and that ethical propositions cannot be empirically tested.

Let me describe an imaginative bit of scientific research I recently directed. It often has been said that it is wrong to torture children, but it seems that no one has proven the point empirically. The Vampire Foundation provided the necessary funds, and I worked with thirty or forty children, carefully recording their EKGs, pulse, and so forth. My thumbscrews gave out at the same time as the hard disk on my computer was filled with data, but I still found no empirical evidence of wrongdoing.

The point of this Gothic story is that scientific research tells us what *is* and not what *ought* to be. One might argue that the society that tortures its children will not survive. Such an argument *assumes* that survival is a value—something that cannot be proven empirically. Science has provided us with much, but it will give us an ethic on the same day that it gives us a square circle.

The fourth point: The modern synthesis (neo-Darwinism) has clearly dominated biology for the past forty years and it continues to do so. But, as Freeman Dyson has pointed out, science does not speak with a single voice. A number of significant biologists have questioned the neo-Darwinian synthesis from the viewpoint of stasis and the rapidity of evolutionary change. For them, the eye is not quite so expected as Dr. Wilson suggested. Pierre Grasse, long the holder of a chair in evolution at the Sorbonne, claims that the probability that copy errors in DNA molecules would lead to the eye is less than that dust blown by the wind would reproduce a drawing of Durer. As for me, I would be unwilling to explain the eye by introducing the "God of the gaps"—God as explanation for the gaps in our knowledge. But, neither would I be ready to rule him out. There are significant gaps in our knowledge of the origin and development of life, and both scientists and theologians should allow them to remain gaps. The gaps are openings that allow room for wonder—something both scientists and theologians need.

In summary: (1) I do not understand a materialist metaphysics that includes—or can include—a natural theology. (2) Intellectual dialogue is possible only if each of the parties has a partial vision of the truth, yet Dr. Wilson seems to allow no truth content to (traditional) religion. His objection is that religion is an enabling mechanism for survival. Perhaps it is, but this in no way undercuts its truth claim. (3) Neither a materialist metaphysic nor the empirical method can give or prove an ethic. (4) There are significant ambiguities and gaps in our understanding of life, and these should be acknowledged.

Discussion

BISHOP HUBBARD: Fr. King has certainly mounted a number of interesting challenges to Dr. Wilson's paper. Let's hear from some of our small groups.

BISHOP EGAN: Our group took issue, in some ways, with Dr. Wilson's presentation. It was felt that he is not in a position with his analysis to explain adequately altruism or variations in human behavior. Likewise, it was thought that his observations on incest prove very little. While it may be true that natural selection biases us against incest, this does not preclude the possibility that religious insight or other factors operate to move us in the same direction.

In our group, we discussed *Humanae Vitae* at some length. One member suggested that the issue of the unitive versus the procreative purpose of sex has a long tradition in Catholic thought. For example, in April 1944, the Holy Office laid out the relationship between the two purposes quite clearly. Even the 1918 *Code of Canon Law* addressed the matter. Dr. Wilson's insight into the unitive purpose does not, therefore, seem to be a new contribution on this subject, at least for Catholics.

DR. FREDERICK LAWRENCE: Our group began by stressing the positive, namely, that Dr. Wilson's approach joins the natural law tradition in looking for discernible limits, tendencies, and things that are given. This presents a salutary counterforce to forms of voluntarism in other theological traditions, to cultural relativism, and to psychologism. We also admit the need to acknowledge any verifiable instances of genetic conditioning, whether in human or subhuman behavior. There is no use blinding ourselves to fact.

On the critical side, our group objects to what we see as reductionism regarding values. Dr. Wilson proposes survival as the unquestioned sole value. This biological perspective provides no framework for discriminating among all sorts of different values, some of which seem to have little to do with simply maintaining and transmitting life. How, for example, does one account for risk taking or self-sacrifice? It is not enough simply to acknowledge complexity. One must face the hierarchization of values, of the structures to which complexity gives rise.

Dr. Wilson also falls prey to methodological or heuristic reductionism. He seems to be trying to apply methods appropriate for one type of investigation to all of human reality. This effort, though daring and challenging, strikes us as simplistic.

On a somewhat different plane, the scientists in our group emphasized the need for facing the problem of genetic manipulation. We lack a framework for intelligently discussing this problem, which is reaching a critical stage. The purpose of genetic engineering should not be simply prediction and control. One can learn from experience, plan for the future, set policy, and so forth. Thus, there is opportunity for ethical and moral discourse, an opportunity that the geneticists are not adequately addressing.

DR. IRENE SCHULZE: Our group discussed Dr. Wilson's statement: "Although many theologians and lay philosophers like to deny it, I believe that traditional religious belief and scientific knowledge depict the universe in radically different ways." We decided that the statement's validity would depend on which tradition one is considering. There is no good reason to posit a general incompatibility between science and religion. Since they treat different aspects of reality, they cannot be mutually exclusive, in our opinion.

Dr. Wilson makes the point that "our profound impulses are rooted in a genetic heritage common to the entire species." Again, we would ask for a clarification. Does "rooted in" mean "based in," or does it imply that our genes are a total and sufficient explanation of human actions? If the former, we see the chance for an interesting discussion, because it is possible to accept this statement without giving up faith. One can argue that our profound impulses are based in genetic heritage and still believe in God.

We ended by asking ourselves what practical steps the scientific community can take to address religious questions effectively. Many scientists, I among them, question whether scientists should try terribly hard to respond to the challenges that religion poses to scientific thought. Certainly, we don't feel it is reasonable to try to explain religious positions scientifically. On the other hand, we do feel the religious community as represented, for example, by the National Conference of Catholic Bishops, would be well advised to enlist the expertise of scientists and to examine the range of scientific opinion when developing position papers.

BISHOP HUBBARD: Dr. Wilson, do you have any response at this point?

DR. WILSON: I came to learn, and I have learned a great deal already. I think I could write a whole book from the notes I have taken. These critiques have been a real road test. You may know that American and British Marxists raise great objections to sociobiology. But, I never had any problems with them compared to this, because they don't bring God in.

I did want to respond substantively to several remarks Bishop Egan made. First, we do have an explanation for altruism. The genetic basis for altruism has been a central issue in the development of the field of sociobiology and one of its most solidly established principles, particularly through kin selection. I won't go into detail, but we understand far more about altruism now than we did ten years ago. Many of the predictions of the theory of kin selection and other aspects of altruism as they apply to the human species have worked very well so far.

Bishop Egan also suggested that incest avoidance might well have come about, in part, because of religious insight. The evidence is powerfully the other way. The evidence argues strongly for an inborn rule, an inhibition imprinted in human beings between the ages of one and six that is wholly independent of any sense of social morality as far as we can detect. In fact, incest avoidance appears in quite a few societies that have no particular moral formulation about incest. It seems, therefore, that if a relevant moral code does arise, it has been built as a superstructure and reinforcement of that basic process.

Finally, it is certainly news to me that the idea of bonding as a part of sexuality is not new in Catholic theology. I appreciate Bishop Egan's mentioning this. I still wonder, however, how much influence the bonding argument had upon Pope Paul VI. With all due respect, it seems to have had not much. My own misperception of Catholic theology in this matter certainly originated from Paul VI's decision.

Let me mention a few points that Fr. King made. He astutely asked, If the anthropic principle is accepted (as I, personally, am inclined to accept it), how can scientific materialism be truly materialistic?

I have made a distinction between what I call the cosmological and the biological God. Biologists may concede that the universe shows some sort of divine plan or some organization with respect to the fine-tuning of physical laws and apportionment of matter in the universe that we cannot now explain, but they are unable to conceive how a divine plan could have been involved in evolution as we understand it. There is a great technical problem here.

Nevertheless, some of us scientists keep an open mind and want to raise the question continually. It seems to us, though, that the ball is in the court of the philosophers and theologians. I don't see any way of deciding this question except, as I indicated in my presentation, by a process of elimination. Either the materialist approach to evolutionary theory holds all the way, even into the profound study of human spirituality, or it does not. The latter outcome would force us all into a much more determined effort to look for divine or external influence. This search would be forced on us as a scientific enterprise, not a theological one.

But, even if the materialistic explanation holds all the way, through chance and necessity and the neo-Darwinian synthesis, how do we know, as Fr. King suggests, that human evolution is not tracking an unseen goal in a direction we have not detected? How can we show that there is no divine plan or, at least, some external set of ethical principles or precepts that exist like mathematical axioms awaiting discovery? This is precisely the response to sociobiology made not by any theologian of whom I am aware but by a Harvard colleague, the philosopher Robert Nozick. He asks, "How do you know it isn't out there?" Then he tiptoes away, without telling us how we are to find it.

Once again, I think the next move is up to the philosophers and theologians. They must explain, in general, how one finds the divine plan, how one identifies it if it is out there like mathematical relationships. I confess that this is simply beyond me, and I am open to suggestions. How does one determine that it is out there other than by a leap of faith? It seems to me that the naturalistic, evolutionary approach has begun to explain many moral precepts as the outcome of evolution by natural selection, ultimately based upon the survival and continuance of human groups. May this not be an adequate explanation, what you call "necessary and sufficient"?

BISHOP HUBBARD: I invite questions and comments from the floor.

FR. ALBERT S. MORACZEWSKI, OP: I would like to respond to Dr. Wilson regarding the genetic dimensions of our profound impulses. When we think about the moral law and Christian doctrine, we should not see them as if they are something external, something imposed from without by divine fiat like the Ten Commandments. Rather, they are rooted in our very nature. Human actions are called evil because they are evil in themselves; they bring some harm ultimately to the individual, to the community, or to the species.

We can adopt Dr. Wilson's example. Incest avoidance is not just a law imposed from without by Christianity or some other moral system. Rather, experience rooted in our genetic makeup shows that incest is a deleterious practice. Moral regulation is not a question of either/or; both genetics and religious reflection contribute. The Ten Commandments articulate what could be known from analysis of human society. Our genes determine our biological makeup, but they do not thereby determine every aspect of our individual actions.

Take another example, the story of the Good Samaritan, where three individuals see a man lying hurt by the wayside. The priest and the Levite pass on, while the Good Samaritan responds altruistically. If we say that altruism is rooted in human nature, we must admit that all three travelers had a genetic disposition toward that virtue. Yet, only one helped the wounded man. What made the difference? If it was not something in common that made the difference, it had to be something individual. One could argue that the biographical experience of each of the three was different and accounted for their actions. But, the evidence can also lead to the conclusion that, while there is an altruistic root in human nature, it is not fully determinative. That is where free choice comes in. The fact that we have a predisposition doesn't force us to respond to it here and now or to respond in a rigidly determined way.

So, we have a combination of factors. There are the genetic component shared in common; the psychosocial environment, which modifies the way the genetic component is expressed; and, finally, free choice, which enables an individual, in spite of the genetic and psychosocial elements, to respond in a way not fully determined by his or her previous experience or genetic makeup. It is this realm of free choice, I think, that is critical in moral behavior.

DR. JEROME LEJEUNE: I was very glad to hear Dr. Wilson treat *Humanae Vitae* in the light of sociobiology. If I understand his argument correctly, he suggests that suspending fertility will increase bonding between parents and increase the security of their children. A very widespread experiment has been run that seems to contradict his claim, however. The experiment has been conducted in the United States, England, France, Italy, Spain, Germany, Denmark, Switzerland, Norway, and many other countries, and its results are evident. Abortion for the elimination of the unborn child has been voted in only those countries where more than twenty percent of the women of child-bearing age were taking toxic contraceptives. It, therefore, seems clear that the use of toxic contraceptives does not lead to improved security for the children. Thus, *Humanae Vitae*, with its emphasis on natural methods of family planning, is vindicated on purely sociobiological principles.

DR. BELA PIACSEK: Dr. Wilson, I have some trouble thinking of human behavior strictly as the product of an evolutionary process. Some human action doesn't seem explainable in terms of the general behavioral principles I see operating in other biological organisms: the preservation of the self, the drive to pass on DNA, and the preservation of the species. For example, Why do we care for the elderly? Where is the advantage? There is no question of self-preservation, no passing on of DNA, no advantage to the species. The behavior doesn't make sense as a product of biological evolution. Nevertheless, both individuals and society care for the elderly because it is considered morally right.

DR. PATRICK BYRNE: I thought one of the most important questions Fr. King put to Dr. Wilson had to do with the value of human life. Dr. Wilson mentioned brother-sister incest and a number of other moral issues on which he thinks sociobiology can offer firm scientific knowledge. From the perspective of sociobiology, the value of a practice such as incest avoidance is that it promotes and protects the survival of the human species. Fr. King asked, however, how science knows that the survival of the human race is a value. After all, evolution is an explanation of extinction as well as survival.

DR. WILSON: Let me respond to Dr. Lejeune's comments first. Correct me if I misconstrue you. Are you saying that in many European countries there is a positive correlation between numbers of children and family stability?

DR. LEJEUNE: I said that European governments have approved abortion—that is, rejection of the child already conceived—only in countries where more than twenty percent of the women of child-bearing age were taking the pill. So, we know by experiment that taking the pill is negatively correlated with the protection of the progeny.

DR. WILSON: You are saying, then, that where artificial contraception becomes more common, abortion becomes more common. Thus, the rearing of conceived offspring becomes less likely. Fair enough. My point, however, was somewhat different. Without descending into the black hole of a discussion of abortion, let me repeat that once children are born, they are likely to be looked after more carefully and brought to maturity more securely if their family has not experienced unlimited expansion. Whether or not I would agree with your comment depends on how one defines "children." Many consider abortion just another form of birth control.

DR. LEJEUNE: I am concerned with biological reality. Abortion means fewer people. You cannot argue that something is beneficial in an evolutionary sense if it decreases the number of progeny. The survival of the progeny is certainly at issue. If the children are not born, however, they cannot survive.

DR. WILSON: I challenge the implications of your statement. The Chinese and other Asiatic peoples have used abortion—this is an observation, not an argument for abortion—as a primary means of birth control. Yet, these cultures are identified with a reverence for the family and with devoting extraordinary care to offspring. This may be another issue; perhaps, we are not in such disagreement.

In any case, throughout much of human history there has been a real advantage to maximizing fertility because the mortality rate, particularly under relatively primitive conditions, was so high as to balance a high birthrate. We are now in a new situation where the mortality rate has dropped very substantially. At the same time, methods of controlling fertility have improved. Thus, as in the case of the People's Republic of China, some kind of morally based population control has to be instituted.

Let me turn to some of the other questions that have been raised. Why care for the elderly? I don't want to engage in "Just So" stories; an imaginative evolutionary biologist can invent good adaptive explanations for nearly anything. The issue of caring for the elderly has received some scholarly attention, though it is admittedly rather speculative. In most human societies throughout human history, old people were relatively scarce and a valuable resource. Even today, in many primitive societies like that of the Australian aborigines, the elderly are the repositories of special knowledge on, for example, the existence of distant water holes; old lineages and kinship relations; and reciprocal arrangements that can be drawn upon in time of emergency. Moreover, in many societies, the elderly traditionally train the children in tribal lore. Since the aged have made long and deeply imbedded contributions to society, they certainly do have adaptive value. Primitive people do not discard the elderly as we do by warehousing them in inadequate nursing homes.

Why do we consider the survival of the human species an intrinsic value? I think the desire to preserve our own lives or the lives of those to whom we are closely bonded by love—our families and tribes—is the deepest trait one can find in human beings and animals. I know of no species that ever showed any tendency whatsoever to self-destruct. If there is any single value that is fundamental to all of life, it is the struggle to stay alive as a species, as a particular line of DNA.

HUMAN WISDOM
AND DIVINE WISDOM

Homily Delivered at a Mass for Conference Participants

SPEAKER
Most Rev. Edmund C. Szoka
Archbishop of Detroit

READINGS
1 Corinthians 2:1-10
Matthew 5:13-16

Readings

1 CORINTHIANS 2:1-10

As for myself, brothers, when I came to you I did not come proclaiming God's testimony with any particular eloquence or "wisdom." No, I determined that while I was with you I would speak of nothing but Jesus Christ and him crucified. When I came among you it was in weakness and fear, and with much trepidation. My message and my preachings had none of the persuasive force of "wise" argumentation, but the convincing power of the Spirit. As a consequence, your faith rests not on the [human] wisdom . . . but on the power of God.

There is, to be sure, a certain wisdom which we express among the spiritually mature. It is not a wisdom of this age, however, nor of the rulers of this age, who are [people] headed for destruction. No, what we utter is God's wisdom: a mysterious, a hidden wisdom. God planned it before all ages for our glory. None of the rulers of this age knew the mystery; if they had known it, they would never have crucified the Lord of glory. Of this wisdom it is written:

> "Eye has not seen, ear has not heard,
>   nor has it so much as dawned on [you]
>   what God has prepared for those
>   who love him."

Yet God has revealed this wisdom to us through the Spirit. The Spirit scrutinizes all matters, even the deep things of God.

MATTHEW 5:13-16

You are the salt of the earth. But what if salt goes flat? How can you restore its flavor? Then it is good for nothing but to be thrown out and trampled underfoot.

You are the light of the world. A city set on a hill cannot be hidden. [People] do not light a lamp and then put it under a bushel basket. They set it on a stand where it gives light to all in the house. In the same way, your light must shine before [all] so that they may see goodness in your acts and give praise to your heavenly Father.

Today's readings and the theme of the conference would suggest that I offer a few reflections on the relationship between science and religion or, framed in the categories of the readings, reflections on human wisdom and divine wisdom. Much like Paul, in today's first reading, I do not come to you proclaiming any earthly or scientific wisdom. Rather, what I utter is "God's wisdom: a mysterious, a hidden wisdom."

It is altogether fitting that this conference take place in Detroit; it is a Renaissance city, a city that has had to rise from the ashes of its own suffering and be transformed time after time. When thinking of the connection between science and religion, between human and divine wisdom, it is only natural that we should remember the Renaissance. Historically, it was that moment of the Renaissance that marked the beginning of a separation of science and religion. The emergent science of the Renaissance made humanity the measure of all things; its thrust was to suggest humanity's radical autonomy. The spirit of the Renaissance was, of course, a reemergence of the same spirit that had dominated the classical world. The Corinthians of old, whom Paul was addressing in today's epistle, were people who prided themselves on their own achievement. Human reason was the highest possible authority.

Paul came, however, proclaiming a different kind of wisdom. He spoke of a wisdom of the spirit: "The Spirit [that] scrutinizes all matters, even the deep things of God." While the Greeks prided themselves on their *techne*, their skill and control of the universe, Paul offered faith. The Greeks strove for the ideal of human progress, but Paul dared to criticize the cultural values inherent in their system. He reminded them that human values only become fully "human" in the light of the wisdom of God's Spirit, for it is God who created all things. Only in the light of His Spirit does any earthly reality make sense or take on an ultimate meaning.

It is significant that in the reading from First Corinthians, Paul speaks of God's wisdom as "mysterious." Perhaps a brief reflection on the word *mystery* will lend understanding to the message of Paul as well as to our conference. *Mystery* in its Greek sense comes from the terms *mus* and *statis*, "a covering of the mouth." A mystery was an experience, a ritual that one could not share with someone who was not initiated into the rite. Paul could not articulate the inner truth of the mystery of God's wisdom, the spiritual power and meaning of human activity, unless a person chose to take the risk of being initiated into the belief system of Christianity. So it was that mystery came to be translated into the Latin as *sacramentum* or *oath*. A mystery was a sacrament, a sign of a deeper reality.

Herein rests the application for us. As Catholic Christians, we exult in the Incarnation. We believe that all creation has the potential to reveal the presence of God; we live in a world that is sacramental. There is no mystery of human life that does not, in some way, reveal the mystery of God himself. As a sacramental people of God, we see the goodness of the world, science and technology, but we are called to consecrate it and raise it to a fuller level of meaning. We believe in mystery. We exult in mystery. But, not the mysteries of the ancient cultic religions of Paul's time. No, we exult in a mystery of love. We believe in a mystery made manifest in our world, a mystery revealed in the cross of Jesus Christ. As St. Paul explains: "None of the rulers of this age knew the mystery; if they had known it, they would never have crucified the Lord of glory."

In our day, as in St. Paul's, scientists and theologians together struggle to face the riddle of the mystery of life and death. As Catholic Christians, we believe that the mysteries of this earth only make sense in light of the mystery of Jesus, who is truly the wisdom of God. The Council fathers of Vatican II state this connection very beautifully in *Gaudium et spes:*

> The truth is that only in the mystery of the incarnate Word does the mystery of [humanity] take on light. . . .

> Pressing upon the Christian, to be sure, are the need and the duty to battle against evil through manifold tribulations and even to suffer death. But, linked with the paschal mystery and patterned on the dying Christ, [the Christian] will hasten forward to resurrection in the strength which comes from hope.

> All this holds true not only for Christians, but for all [people] of good will in whose hearts grace works in an unseen way. For, since Christ died for all . . . , and since the ultimate vocation of [humanity] is in fact one, and divine, we ought to believe that the Holy Spirit in a manner known only to God offers to [everyone] the possibility of being associated with this paschal mystery.

> Such is the mystery of [humanity], and it is a great one, as seen by believers in the light of Christian revelation. Through Christ and

in Christ, the riddles of sorrow and death grow meaningful. Apart from His gospel, they overwhelm us . . . (no. 22).

It is the Christian vocation, today as in Paul's day, to proclaim this mystery: everything of this earth contains within it the potential to reveal the presence of God's wisdom and love. Nothing human is foreign to the Church. Every human endeavor—whether of science or art—is a means of proclaiming and manifesting the divine mystery. Is this not what Jesus is explaining in today's passage from Matthew's Gospel? Jesus reminds the community that they are called to be salt and light. In other words, Jesus takes this message one step further. Not only do the elements of creation proclaim the presence of God but Christians themselves are to be the mysteries, the living signs of God's presence.

How is a Christian to be a sign, a source of light in a world that in many ways favors the darkness? How is a Christian to retain the preservative power of salt in the midst of a world infected with the decay of self-centered interest? How is a Christian to be like salt, which gives flavor in the midst of a world that has so often chosen the bland, flavorless value of total social conformity? A Christian can accomplish this mission in three ways or, more precise, by the specific exercise of three qualities or virtues.

The first necessary requirement for a Christian to live the mystery of God's presence is to recognize the limitation of human wisdom and technology. While pure science is something good and worthy, there is a danger in today's world of giving a priority to technology for its own sake; today's world stresses the ultimate value of production and possessions. As our Holy Father has reminded us in his encyclical *On Human Labor*, the human person must have priority over work. The human person will be truly valued over technological advances only if the Christian recognizes and proclaims the fundamental limitation of all human wisdom. As Pope John Paul II so beautifully pointed out in his November 1979 Address to the Pontifical Academy of Sciences: "Humility creates a climate favorable to dialogue between the believer and the scientist; it calls for the enlightenment of God, already known or still unknown, but loved in either case as by one who humbly seeks the truth." When we recognize and proclaim our limits, at that very moment we free science of a self-imposed tyranny, and we rightfully acknowledge our status as creatures constantly in need of our Creator.

The second virtue necessary for Christians to be light and salt in today's world, to be instruments for the widsom of God, is the virtue of courage. Paul acknowledges in First Corinthians, chapter 2, that when he came among the Corinthians it was "in weakness and fear, and with much trepidation." Nonetheless, convinced by the power of the Spirit, Paul dared to proclaim this mystery of God's love. St. Thomas Aquinas taught that courage is the mean between the two extremes of timidity and rashness. The Christian cannot be afraid to be present in the world, to learn and understand contemporary technology, but he must always be ready to challenge it.

The third and final quality necessary for any Christian to become salt and light, to merge science and religion, is the gift of gratitude. If the Christian courageously acknowledges all wisdom and all gifts as coming from God, then he will rightly give praise and thanks to God. Notice how Jesus concludes today's Gospel: "so that they may see goodness in your acts and give praise to your heavenly Father." The Christian's efforts in science or religion are part of a response of gratitude for all that God has done.

I began today's homily by a reference to Detroit, the Renaissance city. The Renaissance is a rebirth, a metamorphosis, a transformation. For salt and light to be effective, they must undergo a transformation of their very structure. For this city to be reborn, it too must be transformed. If our country, our Church, and our world are to be renewed, it will only be by the transformation of each one of us. As we recognize the limits of our wisdom, work with courage to use the technology at our disposal, and constantly give thanks to God for all these gifts, we will ourselves be transformed by the very experience of our daily human efforts. May both scientists and theologians be true to their vocations, which ultimately converge: to discover, to proclaim, and to live the mystery of the wisdom of God.

THE SCIENCE-VALUES RELATION: IMPACT OF THE CONSCIOUSNESS REVOLUTION

PRESIDER
Most Rev. Dale J. Melczek
Auxiliary Bishop of Detroit

SPEAKER
Dr. Roger W. Sperry
Trustees Professor of Psychobiology Emeritus
California Institute of Technology

RESPONDENT
Rev. Joseph A. Bracken, SJ
Professor of Theology
Xavier University (Cincinnati)

DISCUSSION

Dr. Roger W. Sperry*

As a scientist, my world outlook and beliefs about both human and nonhuman nature underwent a major conversion during the mid-1960s. Long-trusted principles had proclaimed a complete scientific explanation of brain function and behavior—and all human nature—to be possible in strictly physiological or physicochemical terms, with no reference to conscious subjective experience. These principles, which had always seemed to be logically airtight and irrefutable, were discovered to be based, in fact, on a logical flaw or shortcoming. A loophole was found.

As a result, I renounced my earlier views in favor of a new mentalist paradigm in which the traditionally rejected subjective mental and spiritual qualities of the conscious mind were interpreted to play an active, functional, causal role in brain processing. In this new "mentalist" scheme, subjective conscious states, as emergents of brain action, became ineliminable causal constructs in scientific explanation. This meant that my outlook in science must be reversed to include conscious experience among the legitimate causes of behavior.

The new reasoning was introduced to the National Academy of Sciences and to psychology in the late 1960s. And, by the mid-1970s, psychology too had reversed its position on consciousness and switched from behaviorism to a new mentalist or cognitivist paradigm. In what follows, I shall be speaking from the standpoint of this paradigm shift in behavioral science in general, not from my personal philosophy—though I take the two to be identical in terms of underlying principles. For our present purposes, however, it is important to emphasize the basis in mainstream psychology, not in personal opinion. What is involved essentially is a shift to a new form of causal determinist, a shift that I hold to be a move toward

---

*Most of this paper was read for Dr. Sperry by his wife, Norma, because his speech is slowed by an advancing neuromotor condition.

a more valid conceptual foundation for all science, not just psychology.

The answer to the question, "Is there convergence between science and religion?" seems from the standpoint of psychology to be a definite and emphatic "Yes!" Over the past fifteen years, these changed foundational concepts have brought radical revisions in our scientific descriptions of the nature of human nature and the psyche. The resultant views today are much more palatable and compatible for theology than were those of the behaviorist-materialist era. Where religious belief and scientific belief formerly stood in direct conflict, even to the point of being mutually exclusive, one now sees promise for a new compatibility, perhaps even harmony.

At the risk of being repetitive, it will help to say a little more about these developments on which the convergence in question directly depends. The developments I refer to are not something vague, abstract, or obscure; nor are they a matter of wishful thinking. The swing in psychology from behaviorism to mentalism (or cognitivism) during the 1970s is a widely recognized and well-documented shift of majority opinion and practice—a true paradigm shift to a new conceptual framework for the science of behavior. In the early 1970s, the objective radical behaviorism that had dominated psychology for over half a century gave way rather abruptly to a new, more subjective explanatory framework called mentalism or cognitivism. In short, this change can be seen to provide science and all of us with a new philosophy, a new outlook, a new way of understanding and explaining ourselves and the world.

The contents of conscious experience, long banned from scientific explanation by rigorous objective behaviorist and materialist principles, have now made a strong comeback. Subjective mental states and events such as mental images, feelings, thoughts, memories, and other introspective phenomena, formerly renounced as nonvalid and useless for objective scientific explanation, have become widely accepted today as explanatory causal constructs. Described by some psychologists as a "deep conceptual conversion," this turnabout in doctrine is commonly referred to as the *consciousness* or *cognitive* or *mentalist* revolution and has also been called the *humanist* or *third* revolution (the first two having been associated with John Watson and Sigmund Freud). In effect, the conception of conscious experience in brain function and behavior was turned around from that of a nonfunctional, noncausal epiphenomenon, or parallel aspect or byproduct of brain function, to that of an integral, ineliminable directive working force.

A new solution to the age-old mind-brain problem is involved, as well as a revised form of causal determinism. Also, our concepts in neuroscience of the working of the physical brain and of the kinds of governing forces that are in control undergo substantial revision. Where previously science had relied exclusively on objective neuronal activity, biophysics, biochemistry, and, eventually, quantum mechanics, the scientific account now includes subjective qualities as explanatory constructs. The full range of the contents and qualities of the world of inner experience have not only been reinstated but are now given primacy over the more basic physicochemical forces. As emergents of brain activity, the higher-level mental states are conceived to interact causally at their own level and, concomitantly, to exert control from above downward over their constituent neuronal events at the same time that they are being determined by them.

The invoked principle of causal control from above downward in organizational hierarchies—later dubbed *downward causation* by Donald Campbell, Sir Karl Popper, and others—can be applied at all levels throughout science. The new outlook says that we and our world are more than just swarms of atoms, electrons, and protons. The higher holistic properties and qualities of nature to which the brain responds—the colors, the forms, the weights, the sounds, along with things such as purpose, intentionality, and caring in human and social activity—all become just as real and causal for science as are the atoms and molecules on which they depend— and they cannot be reduced to quantum mechanics. The outcome is a renunciation of the quantum mechanics philosophy that has dominated science for over half a century (but not, of course, of quantum physics *per se*). Among other consequences, much of our traditional reasoning regarding the polarization of science and religion, freedom and determinism, fact and value, "is" and "ought," becomes obsolete, with new possibilities opened for a convergence of theological and scientific thought.

It seems fair to say that, prior to this mentalist revolution, that is, up through the 1960s, mainstream science and religion actually had stood to one another as archenemies. All through the behaviorist-mentalist era, science had been upholding an impersonal, value-devoid, physically driven cosmos governed by chance and quantum mechanics. This strictly physically determined cosmos was conceived to be ultimately lacking in purpose, caring, higher meaning, morality, and other attributes that are essential and, indeed, vital to the concerns of religion. Things such as subjective value, purpose, and meaning—if they existed at all—were supposed to be only epiphenomena of brain activity, best ignored in scientific explanation since they, supposedly, in no way changed the course of events in the real world, either in the brain or in the universe at large.

The foregoing characterization of pre-1970s science and religion as "archenemies" may appear a bit harsh in view of seeming exceptions such as, for example, Ralph Burhoe's Institute of Religion in an Age of Science (IRAS) and the associated *Zygon Journal of Religion and Science*. It is presupposed, however, that we are here discussing mainstream science and religion. It has long been a stated policy for IRAS and *Zygon* that the attempt to join science and religion must be based on solid mainstream science, not on fringe activities and minority opinions that might try to pass as science. For this reason, the Burhoe project was constrained to try to merge religion with the prevailing materialist, reductionist doctrines of mainstream science. This, of course, meant trying to merge religion with radical behaviorism, the selfish gene concept, quantum mechanics philosophy, and all the other reductive, mechanistic, deterministic views upheld in traditional materialist philosophy. Despite good intentions and valiant attempts in this direction over several decades, this project never really succeeded from the standpoint of religion. As one theologian jocularly summarized the effort recently: "With friends like these, who needs enemies!"

The actual relation of religion to mainstream materialist science seems to have been more realistically assessed by the council of the National Academy of Sciences when, in 1981, they issued the following resolution, quoted in the Academy's booklet *Science and Creationism*: "Religion and science are separate and mutually exclusive realms of human thought, presentation of which in the same context leads to misunderstanding of both scientific theory and religious belief." In other words, acceptance of the reductive physicalist beliefs traditionally upheld in scientific materialism logically destroys the kinds of beliefs upheld in religion and vice versa.

As already stressed, this mutually exclusive "archenemy" status is, today, a thing of the past—at least in behavioral science—thanks to the consciousness revolution. We used to be faced, in the last analysis, with a choice between two mutually exclusive conceptions of ultimate reality: the spiritual-religious and the physical-scientific frameworks for belief. The new mentalist paradigm introduces a third choice. Described as a midway compromise, this new outlook on reality combines formerly antithetical features from both sides of the old spiritual-physical dichotomy into a new world-view synthesis. The new outlook integrates the physical with the metaphysical (what Dr. Wilson has referred to as materialism vs. transcendentalism), positivistic thought with phenomenology. It accepts subjectively experienced mental and spiritual qualities as autonomous causal realities. At the same time, however, it denies that these mental-spiritual phenomena can exist separately in an unembodied form apart from the functioning brain.

To better understand the new outlook, it will help to view it in relation to the changes called for in our concepts of causation. The traditional assumption in behaviorist psychology, like that in neuroscience, physics, biology, chemistry, and all the natural sciences, supposed everything to be determined from below upward, following the course of evolution. In this "microdeterminist" view, all brain function is determined by, and can be explained in terms of, brain physiology or neuronal activity. In turn, the neuronal activity can be explained in terms of biophysics and biochemistry and so on, everything being determined and accounted for eventually in terms of subatomic physics and quantum mechanics—or some even more elemental "theory of everything."

The new mentalism rejects this exclusive, reductive microdeterminist reasoning and replaces it with another. The new outlook accepts the control from below upward but claims this is not the whole story, that a full explanation requires that one also takes into account controls exerted from above downward by the higher level properties of a system. This control is referred to as "macro," "molar," or "emergent" determinism. It is the failure to recognize this downward control, along with dualist explanations in theology, that have made religious and scientific belief seem mutually exclusive. With reductionist fallacies now corrected in the new macrodeterminism, there seems no logical reason why scientific belief cannot be fused with religious belief, so long as dualist views are avoided (which, I am told, is no great problem in contemporary theology).

Psychology's new mentalist paradigm resolves the old free-will issue by retaining determinism—both "micro" and "macro"—in such a way that the antecedent causes determining one's willed actions include subjective wants, values, and other mental aspects that make up the cognitive self. Thus, from the standpoint of mentalist doctrine, as from that of common experience, one does what one subjectively chooses or *wants* to do.

Mentalism also erases much of the old antithesis between scientific fact and values. Subjective values become objective causes of behavior, not excluded any longer from scientific explanation. In addition, the cosmology and world view of science are reformed in ways that no longer destroy values. Further, our current concepts of cognitive processing make it logically and theoretically possible to go from *is* to *ought*, rendering the "naturalistic fallacy" itself fallacious. The combined result is a new era in the science-values relation.

REMAINING ISSUES

We turn now to other areas of agreement and disagreement between science and religion. I hope most of us will agree at the start on at least one general presupposition: namely, that human belief systems, along with their attendant values and moral priorities, have tremendous power in shaping social policy and the course of world events and (especially with the explosive increase in the human impact) that human beliefs will be a major, if not the key, factor in determining the future for all life on our planet. From the standpoint of brain processing, the central importance of the belief system as a determinant of behavior and decision making at all levels can hardly be overrated. Religious, philosophic, and ideologic beliefs, in particular, incorporate or imply a world view or life-goal framework that then ultimately determines the public judgment of how things ought to be in the world—the cultural sense of value and conceptions of right and wrong.

A crucial remaining issue that is brought into new focus by the mentalist paradigm can be stated as follows: In forming ideologic or religious belief, is it any longer necessary and/or desirable to go beyond the limits of present knowledge and empirical verification? In other words, do we put our faith in the kind of truth limited by reason and the domains within which scientific and religious belief are in accord? Or, do we reach beyond into other realms? The answer, of course, is critical to the treatment of many other issues.

Until the 1970s, there was little choice; theology could hardly depend on scientific doctrine that, in the final analysis, was mutually exclusive and incompatible with its own aims. In addition, it has often been said that science, at its best, does not go far enough to satisfy the ultimate concerns of religion.

In our changed situation today, however, new reasons can be seen for basing our belief systems—at least at the social level and for purposes of legislation—firmly within the bounds of empirical verification where science can lend support. Publication trends of the past dozen years show increasingly that, with the new paradigm and other advances, one can arrive at a very workable theology or value-belief system that is sound and consistent and has competitive appeal and credibility—all staying within bounds acceptable to science.

The principal argument, however, relates to the power of belief systems in determining social values and the future. It says, in effect, that if we risk mistakes in this critical area or even fail to correct past errors, it could easily mean our finish. If we do not succeed soon in finding a theology that will protect the biosphere, and if we do not find a neutral "common denominator" belief system and ethic on which most nations and most cultures and faiths can agree, then very shortly we may not have any nations or theologies or sciences to worry about—or even any biosphere. In today's scenario, the issue of survival (or better, of quality survival) logically takes overwhelming precedence over all other moral imperatives.

Current efforts, based mainly in science and technology, to cope with mounting global ills represent a losing battle. Only a major overhaul in the existing social and moral order can be expected to provide a sustainable civilization. The key, I believe, lies in the kinds of values and moral priorities that would result from a merger of religion with the new science. The beliefs and values that would logically result are in tune with world reality. Expressed through social policy and legislation, these values would preserve and enhance the biosphere instead of destroying it. Building on the neutral universality and credibility of scientific truth, they would also provide a basic, common-core global ethic for world government or, at least, for a world security system to control nuclear and other metanational global threats.

Finally, in closing, it may be emphasized that, today, to opt for putting our faith in the kind of truth supported by science does not at all diminish the need for theology. Most scientists, caught up in the minute details of specific problems, couldn't care less about the value implications or ultimate bearing of their discoveries. Even when they do, the value-belief implications involve a highly complex discipline, one that needs specialists of its own—not to mention all the implementation aspects in practical application.

Initially, science and theology started out together in search of answers. Now, the way seems to be opened again for a reunion in the search for a more intimate understanding of the forces that made and move the universe and created humanity and for ultimate guideline beliefs to live and govern by.

ADDENDUM

In attempting to go further into some of the more specific issues on which religion and science might still differ, despite the new "macro" paradigm, I found I did not know enough about the tenets of the different mainline religions—nor even enough about the different contemporary interpretations of Christianity—to define effectively the possible remaining areas of conflict. It seemed better merely to try to list briefly a few of the relevant implications of the new paradigm, leaving it for others more competent in these areas to determine to what extent there may be agreement or conflict.

In general, the new outlook supports a system in which the most sacred things in life are neither reduced to quantum mechanics nor set off apart in another world of existence. Resultant moral priorities are this-worldly and, more important, of a kind that will act to preserve and enhance the long-range quality of our biosphere, as well as to provide a common neutral basis for international, inter-cultural, and interfaith compromise on ethical issues and how things ought to be in the world.

In the eyes of science, humanity's creator becomes the vast creative force system in "evolving nature," which includes human nature. Nature is qualified in this context as "evolving" or "emer-gent" or "creative" because there are destructive forces in nature as well as creative ones.

Evolving nature in macrodeterminist terms involves gradual emergence of increased direction and purpose among the forces that move and govern living things at both collective and individual levels, including an emergent awareness and spirituality in higher brains. Current conceptions of causation rule out the separation of creation and creator. In the perspectives of science, the two are intricately and inextricably interfused and evolve together. The creative force system is, thus, not a static but a dynamic entity that grows and evolves as evolution progresses.

From the standpoint of brain processing, values—including ethical and moral values—are relative to this world's reality. Only the highest good, expressed in the abstract as "implementing God's will" or "enhancing the quality of existence," remains constant. Concrete moral directives for achieving the highest good logically change as reality and world conditions change. Even the sanctity of human life is relative to reality, not absolute.

As human numbers grow, and as human interests and welfare increasingly overwhelm or come into competition and conflict with those of other species, questions arise as to the extent to which humankind should take or be given precedence. This becomes one of the great moral issues of our age. Is this planet primarily or exclusively for humanity, as many claim, or do other species also have "rights"?

It seems ironic that humanity's aspirations for immortality, if maladaptively implemented, could result indirectly in destroying not only our immortality but also our mortal existence, as well as that of numerous other species.

Rev. Joseph A. Bracken, SJ

Given the enormity of the problems facing human beings today, not only to live well but simply to survive on planet Earth, Dr. Roger Sperry's appeal for a new world view that brings together the facts established by the natural and social sciences and the value-laden beliefs traditionally upheld by the great world religions certainly deserves careful consideration. Since I myself have been for some years at work on basically the same project, namely, the creation of a new world view more in line with contemporary self-understanding, I am very pleased to have this opportunity formally to respond to Dr. Sperry.

He suggests, quite properly in my judgment, that such a merger between science and religion will not take place unless proponents of both science and religion rethink the assumptions that have classically held them apart. That is, religion must give up "dependence on dualistic concepts," while science must renounce "much of its traditional materialistic legacy, including decades-old behavioristic, reductionistic, probabilistic, mechanistic, and deterministic principles."[1] As proof that science, for its part, is already moving in that direction, Dr. Sperry cites his own research into the mind/brain relation. Increasingly, the empirical results coming out of that line of work have led him to the conclusion that the reductionist approach of Newtonian science, whereby the existence and activity of entities are exclusively to be explained in terms of the laws governing the existence and activity of their component parts, must be set aside in favor of a new operational premise that he calls "downward causation." Dr. Sperry explains the latter as "the idea that, in the reciprocal interaction of lower and higher levels [within a given organism], the higher laws and forces (once evolved) exert downward causal control over the lower forces. The lower level forces in any entity are enveloped, overwhelmed, and overpowered

---

[1]Roger Sperry, "Changed Concepts of Brain and Consciousness: Some Value Implications," *Zygon Journal of Religion and Science* (March 1985): 44.

by the higher."[2] Applied to brain/mind research, this implies that "the physical and chemical forces in the brain, though still present and operating, are enveloped and programmed by the higher laws and dynamics of conscious and subconscious mental processes."[3] Accordingly, on strictly scientific grounds, Dr. Sperry can allow for freedom of choice and purposeful behavior on the part of human beings, something that would be impossible within a deterministic or behavioristic frame of reference.

Yet, the dialogue between science and religion will not be truly productive, says Dr. Sperry, until theologians rethink the basic beliefs of their traditions in nondualistic terms. Once again, I agree, although I feel obliged to add some qualifications of both a philosophical and theological nature. For example, Dr. Sperry does not seem to be aware of the difference between *pantheism* and *panentheism*. Pantheism proposes that "God" is simply a name for the universe as a functioning ontological totality. In particular, God is to be identified with the laws and forces that hold the universe together from moment to moment. Panentheism, on the other hand, holds that God is immanent in the universe but, at the same time, transcendent to it. The created universe, in other words, exists in and through the power of God; but God's own being and activity are not limited to the creation and preservation of the material world.

As a Christian, I reject the model of pantheism because it runs counter to belief in God as personal, indeed, tripersonal, as I shall explain shortly. But, both as a Christian and as a philosopher/ theologian committed to a process-oriented approach to reality after the manner of Alfred North Whitehead, I endorse panentheism. I believe that, while God and the world are dialectically related so that what happens to creatures likewise impacts on God and affects the divine relationship to those same creatures, God transcends the world. God's own being and activity, in other words, are not intrinsically dependent upon the world of creation. In this respect, I differ from Whitehead for whom God and the world are opposite "poles" within the same cosmic process. Rather, as I make clear in my book *The Triune Symbol*, God is to be understood as a com-

---

[2]Ibid., p. 47.
[3]Roger Sperry, "The Mentalist Paradigm and Ultimate Concern," *Perspectives in Biology and Medicine* (Spring 1986): 418.

munity of three divine persons who share their intersubjective life with all their creatures but, above all, with their rational creatures on an ongoing basis.

Dr. Sperry might well object here that, while scientists are increasingly ready to accept the notion of a "grand orderly design" in the evolution of higher forms of life within the cosmic process,[4] they resist the idea of a Creator God who planned it all from the beginning. There is simply too much scientific evidence for the role of chance in the evolution of species or, indeed, for the interplay of atoms and molecules at lower levels of existence and activity. But, at least in terms of the neo-Whiteheadian scheme that I propose, there is ample room both for spontaneity on the part of the creature (in terms of the "decisions" of "actual entities") and for divine empowerment of the creature to decide in the form of "initial aims" offered by the divine persons. Thus, chance, when understood as the spontaneous self-development of the creature, is not at all incompatible with belief in a Creator God who continually adjusts the divine plan for the salvation of the world to *de facto* occurrences in the created order.

What seems to be needed, then, by way of common ground between the proponents of science and religion is a new metaphysics that will safeguard the traditional beliefs and values of religion and, yet, be compatible with new developments in the natural and social sciences. I will offer a few more illustrations of how the neo-Whiteheadian scheme, alluded to above, might be a first step in that direction.

Last year, in an article for *International Philosophical Quarterly*,[5] I argued that the Whiteheadian category of "society," properly reinterpreted, provides a more satisfactory foundational concept for a new evolutionary cosmology than either the classical concept of substance in Aristotelian-Thomistic metaphysics or the "natural system" notion of philosophers of science such as Ervin Laszlo. A Whiteheadian society, it will be remembered, is a grouping of "actual entities" temporally and, in most cases, also spatially ordered in virtue of what Whitehead calls a "common element of form" or basic pattern of intelligibility inherent in the self-consti-

---

[4] "Changed Concepts," p. 50.

[5] Joseph A. Bracken, "Substance-Society-Natural Systems: A Creative Rethinking of Whitehead's Cosmology," *International Philosophical Quarterly* (1985): 3-13.

tution of each of those same entities.[6] As such, it is more in keeping
with evolutionary theory than the classical concept of substance
since it provides for the continuous emergence of higher-level forms
of order and intelligibility out of the dynamic interrelationship of
lower-level entities as their component "parts." That is, whereas
in Aristotelian metaphysics the form is the preestablished ordering
principle of the component parts of a substance, in this scheme
actual entities by their dynamic interrelation generate, at least in
principle, a new form at every instant. Granted that the change in
the formal structure of a given "society" is very slight from moment
to moment, nevertheless, the fact of evolution is much more readily
accounted for in this scheme than in classical metaphysics, with its
relatively fixed, preestablished forms.

At the same time, the Whiteheadian notion of "society," at least
as I interpret it, seems to be metaphysically better founded than
the concept of a "natural system" in Laszlo's philosophy since it
alone explains how new forms of order and intelligibility (new
"natural systems") come into being and are sustained in existence.
Within Laszlo's scheme, there is a hierarchical grading of natural
systems, with the less complex serving as the parts for the more
complex at each level of existence and activity. But, no metaphysical explanation is offered for the ultimate component parts of
all the systems—the "actual entities" as Whitehead calls them—
that, by their dynamic interrelationship, provide the ontological
basis for the existence and activity of the entire hierarchy of systems.
In addition, since there are different kinds of actual entities in
Whitehead's philosophy, with the more complex, higher-grade actual entities emerging only after the lower-grade actual entities have
reached a definite level of self-organization into societies, his thought
provides a rationale for the gradual emergence of life from nonlife,
animal life from plant life, and rational consciousness from animal
consciousness.

Finally, if the process-oriented equivalent of a "soul" can thereby
be established within the human organism, then it is at least conceivable that religious belief in personal immortality could be rendered intelligible, even if not actually justified, by further studies
in philosophy and psychology. If, as Whitehead claims, there is
within the human brain a "regnant" society of high-grade actual

---

[6]Alfred North Whitehead, *Process and Reality: An Essay in Cosmology*, corr. ed.
by David Griffin and Donald Sherburne (New York: Free Press, 1978), p. 34.

entities that exists both for its own enjoyment and to provide direction for the human organism as a whole, it is at least conceivable that such a society could survive the death of the body and the collapse of its infrastructure in the brain. Whereas previously the society owed its existence and activity to energy sources in the human body, it would now have to be grounded in a higher energy source apart from the body, that is, in the communitarian life of the three divine persons. To explain this last idea in detail would take me well beyond the bounds of this present paper. What I offer here are simply projections for a full-scale metaphysics that, in principle, must be consistent with the evolutionary, this-worldly horizons of contemporary science, yet, at the same time, do justice to the deeply rooted religious aspiration of human beings in this age—as in all previous ages.

Discussion

BISHOP MELCZEK: Do any of our discussion groups have comments to volunteer?

FR. WILLIAM LORI: Our group reached a sort of consensus regarding Dr. Sperry's statement that survival takes precedence over everything else as a value. We agree that the survival of the biosphere is a critical, overarching question and an urgent moral imperative. Having said that, however, we began to talk about the place of individual moral questions and imperatives in the context of this overall, universal problem. We noted that the Church tries to maintain two bodies of moral teaching: a social one, concerned with great issues like preventing nuclear war and preserving the biosphere; and an individual one, emphasizing personal decision making. We sense that there is some common matrix between those two kinds of moral teaching, even if this matrix is not well understood.

DR. ROBERT RUSSELL: We would first like to express our appreciation for the courage Dr. Sperry has shown in critiquing and adjusting the world view that dominated his earlier work. We were moved by his "conversion" and recognize our own responsibility to be very clear about what we are committed to in our traditions and what we need to examine.

Dr. Sperry said: "With reductionistic fallacies now corrected in the new macrodeterminism, there seems no logical reason why scientific belief cannot be fused with religious belief, so long as dualist views are avoided. . . ." We would be inclined to agree with this statement if we are permitted to change a few words; for example, we would substitute *ideas* for *beliefs*. "Scientific belief" strikes us as a curious and, perhaps, unfair term, and "religious belief" may be too general to be useful. If you compare scientific ideas, concepts, or hypotheses to religious ones, on the other hand, there could be a great deal of overlap and mutual elimination and critique.

We were also uneasy with the word *fusion*. We weren't sure what you would get if you fused science and religion; you might only succeed in losing both. However, if some sort of interactive overlap could be constructed, as St. Thomas did with Aristotle, it could trigger a new age as far as critiquing the metaphysics that underlies our theology is concerned. Thomas himself, after all, used Aristotle to critique earlier theologians. It isn't just a matter of selecting and rejecting, but a process of honestly wrestling with the best science, the best philosophy, of our time. A critical examination of theology as it embraces the issues science raises is essential.

We agree with Dr. Sperry that survival is the most urgent issue of our day. Those of us in the fields of moral and philosophical reflection have a special call to embrace the challenge of technology and to examine world crisis. We should also question the focus of survival. Is it individual? Is it the species? Is it the species plus the ecology on which species depends? Is it planet Earth? There is ambiguity in the question of who survives and how survival is defined, and this ambiguity generates some of the misunderstandings and problems in the moral critique of technology.

Our group talked briefly about a way of combining two speakers' ideas. Dr. Dyson eloquently discussed three levels of consciousness: quantum mechanical, human, and cosmic. Dr. Sperry talked about downward causation as a new concept in the analysis of mind/body relations. Is there any sense, we wonder, in which the Cosmic Mind might be the source of downward causation? If so, what would be the locus of that causation? Would it be the universe in the sense that Cosmic Mind could change the future? Or, would downward causation be more local, affecting individual humans? Can mystical experience be interpreted in this light? All very speculative, of course, but interesting.

SR. ROSEMARY DONLEY, SC: Our group raised a number of issues, which I will mention briefly. We also feel moved to issue a caution. While the dialogue between science and religion is certainly important, we must avoid parochialism. This applies not just to the Catholic tradition but to all traditions.

We strongly agree that survival is a most important moral imperative. We discussed the role of charity as a theological concept and noted that ultimate survival for us is the gaining of eternal life. We share a concern with world order, a concern that has to be international. We agree with Dr. Sperry that God is in the universe. But, as Catholics, we have another belief that we do not see as competitive, namely, that God also transcends the universe. In discussing this point, we recognized the importance of not losing sight of our differences. These differences and diversities do not prevent our working together. At the same time, they are very significant when it comes to treatment of final goals such as survival.

We had an interesting discussion on what we mean today by "natural law." Clearly, it is essential that people in our tradition examine the concept of natural law in the light of the findings of modern science. Traditionally, Catholics believe that grace builds upon nature, that grace is not limited by nature. Thus, science must not be allowed to co-opt religion, just as religion is not called to "convert" science.

BISHOP MELCZEK: Any comments on these group reflections?

CARDINAL BERNARD LAW: Let me pick up on what Sr. Donley said just now about natural law, in reference to the quotation from Dr. Sperry's paper regarding the fusion of religious and scientific belief. It seems to me that Dr. Sperry's statement can be understood in terms of natural law, in our classical terminology. This understanding, in turn, offers a basis for a more humane system in dealing with questions of survival.

Science is uniquely qualified to illumine that natural law that develops in terms of human experience. I wonder if the fusion or point of contact Dr. Sperry hopes for is not already present in the Catholic tradition: the concept of natural law may provide a basis for more creative interaction with the scientific community. It may also lay the groundwork for interaction with other world religions, since discussion of natural law does not threaten beliefs that flow out of revelation, out of the teachings of individual religious leaders.

DR. JAMES BLACHOWICZ: Our group spent considerable time discussing reductionism, the effort to treat phenomena at one level as explainable in terms of a lower level. We wondered if there are cases where reductionism does not apply that would be helpful in establishing the autonomy of religion and science. After all, there is no point in discussing the compatibility of religion and science if the two are not autonomous to begin with. Civil engineering is autonomous in that a bridge builder can do the job without knowing atomic physics. Some biologists assert most emphatically that biology is not reducible to chemistry. Is this sort of autonomy helpful in regard to the religion/science question? Granted that a phenotype may depend on a genotype, the genotype is also influenced by the phenotype. That is, genes are what they are because human beings struggle in particular ways in particular environments. There is a kind of downward causation here as well. Are these reflections helpful for our discussion?

It would be helpful to get Dr. Dyson's and Dr. Wilson's reactions to reductionist thought. Is there any legitimate sense in which the data of their respective disciplines cannot be explained in terms of anything else? Can an ethical system's survival be explained by Darwinian principles and, yet, retain an autonomy that a Darwinian would recognize?

BISHOP MELCZEK: Let's hear first from Dr. Sperry, and then from Dr. Dyson and Dr. Wilson.

DR. SPERRY: Most biologists I know teach that biology is molecular and chemical, and they practice what they teach. I'm not sure from your statement whether you are agreeing or disagreeing with that.

DR. BLACHOWICZ: I would support a *de facto* autonomy on the part of biology, without getting into the theoretical question. A biologist can do all sorts of investigations in his or her discipline without having to know chemistry. The chemists in our group took a stronger stance, suggesting that biology is not even theoretically deducible from chemistry. There are emergent laws and principles, they say, that can't be deduced from chemical ones.

DR. SPERRY: Well, good for them. I doubt, though, that this is standard thinking, in general, among chemists. When it comes to relating chemistry to biology, I think we must all agree that to know the chemistry of something biological usually helps enormously for our understanding, prediction, and control. What is at issue are the kinds of conclusions to be drawn therefrom regarding the nature of the forces that control biology. Is the biosphere therefore controlled by the elemental forces of chemistry, or do the vital forces of life, society, and the human spirit have also to be recognized as causal realities in their own form, at their own level?

The situation in modern physics is more complicated, with the old mechanistic views of Newtonian physics being renounced on the basis of seemingly reductionist reasoning in which subatomic properties are extrapolated to "macro" Newtonian realms. I am not sure what physicists would say.

DR. DYSON: Physics contains a variety of diverse disciplines. For example, sciences such as geophysics and astrophysics examine things that are available to observation and that don't change a great deal over time. They deal with the past, especially geophysics. On the other hand, there are sciences such as quantum mechanics that essentially deal with the future. When you discuss a quantum mechanical situation, you are always making probabilistic statements about the future. That is all quantum mechanics can do; you can't talk about the past in quantum mechanical language.

So, yes, there is a great deal of autonomy among the different branches of physics. And it is certainly not useful or fruitful to reduce geophysics to quantum mechanics even if it were possible, which I doubt. Reductionism isn't really an issue for the physicists. We moved beyond that a long time ago.

DR. WILSON: To coin a phrase, "Reductionism is the opiate of the scientist." The triumph of science has come largely through the reductionist enterprise. It has always been accompanied by resynthesis. The ideal of much scientific research has been to take a complex process, to crack it apart into its component units (not always the ultimate units of subatomic particles, but those at the next level of organization down), to characterize those units as real units in such a way that they can be recombined according to certain algorithms, and hence to explain more fully the level at which you started. Reductionism works extremely well as a methodology, especially if combined with a resynthesis that takes into account position effects.

On the other hand, reductionism fails as a philosophy, especially when defined strictly, as I suspect our chemist colleagues are doing. A strict reductionism holds that everything can be explained by simple reference to the constituent units studied on their own terms, without reference to the higher systems into which they can be assembled.

Dr. Sperry's presentation was on target, in my opinion, all the way through. But, I was somewhat puzzled by his use of words like *reductionism* and *materialism* and even *mentalism* in a fashion that evoked old wars and values. I would have benefitted from some concrete examples. If you will forgive me, Dr. Sperry, I will suggest one, just to show how the emergent explanation is beginning to take hold as part of cognitive science.

We have always thought of dreams as quite ethereal and intangible, yet, the physical equipment involved in producing one is incredibly complex. Let's glance at the phenomena that may be concatinated in the dream process to distinguish explanations that recognize higher organization and top-down control from mere reductionist explanations at the level of neurons. There are somewhere between ten and one hundred billion neurons in the brain, each of which has somewhere on the order of one to ten thousand neural connections. The brain is the most awesome concrete object of which we are aware in the whole universe. When you go to sleep, you shut down most of your sensory systems. You enter a REM period. At this point, long neurons in the brain stem fire upward into the cortical area, where are located immense numbers of neurons that form the seat of long-term memory.

Now, we are in a process that might be called "top-down organization." These long-term memory neurons are activated, and they feed imagery down into the short-term memory centers and the seats of consciousness. (Don't ask me to define this process precisely, but it is a mapping and scenario-making procedure that occurs with extreme rapidity.) The particular long-term memories involved, and hence the imagery they create, are affected by a number of things, including your emotional state, whether you had too much food the evening before, and so on. But, a large amount of random—or at least not easily explained—imagery appears in fragments. The mind has an extraordinary capacity to make stories. This is what consciousness is all about, a constant scenario building back and forth through time. The stories will make a certain amount of sense, and they will involve certain feelings. The mind flashes through a story, a reconstruction of reality.

The full biological meaning of the dream and its adaptive significance are not fully understood. Reductionist scientists feel, however, that we can explain the dream state, which has such an extraordinary importance for culture and human feeling, ultimately at the neuronal level. The reductionist hopes to discover reality by explicating the cell biology of the neurons. Dr. Sperry maintains, and I agree, that you cannot begin to understand something like dream imagery simply by cataloging and studying all the neurons. You have to understand the hierarchic control, this feed-down from a higher to a lower level.

Forgive this long-winded account. I may have scandalized Dr. Sperry and others who know neurobiology better than I do. I wanted to try to reconcile the validity of reductionist methodology with the new holistic, cognitive mode of assembling information and recreating patterns.

DR. SPERRY: Sociobiology seems also to have undergone a conversion. It is good news indeed to learn of this potential support for top-down control. Such views are still far outweighed in science at large by traditional "micro" reasoning and much in need of any support that arises.

I think the issue of reductionism is very much alive, even in physics, at least in reference to quantum mechanics. When quantum mechanics came along and proved to be superior to classical physical theory for subatomic phenomena, there was a natural sweeping out of the old in favor of the new. The idea took hold that quantum theory subsumes, includes, and replaces classical theory, a conclusion that antireductionist thinking would oppose. Most physicists still make this argument very strongly, pointing to mathematical equations. I suspect, however, that these equations also reflect classical physics. They contain functions that, if reduced to zero, permit the equation to work for classical physics. But, this eliminates quantum theory. Both theories work, but at different levels.

FR. MCMULLIN: Reductionism has been at the center of philosophic discussion for quite a long time. Let me go back to the seventeenth century for a moment. Descartes proposed a physics where all action is the result of contact between bodies, push and pull. No other form of action is permitted. That is, obviously, a highly reductionist scheme; gravitational attraction over distance is eliminated, for example. Descartes rejected gravity because he thought direct contact could handle everything, even the movement of the planets. Newton had to oppose this simplistic physics in favor of a richer notion.

In the nineteenth century, there was a great deal of interest in how color reveals itself in terms of optical frequencies. It became clear that Newtonian mechanics was insufficient to explain a very basic feature of our world, namely, color. A long sequence of events between the 1860s and the 1920s led to a new mechanics that used quantum notions that did not appear in the older physics. To explain color, you need quantum mechanics.

Dr. Wilson spoke of methodological reductionism. You can take a theory such as Descartes' "action by direct contact" or Newton's "gravitation" and you push it as far as it will go. Yet, there is a different, stronger kind of ontological reductionism that claims that only certain kinds of entity exist and that all things are theoretically explainable in terms of these entities.

This stronger reductionism, which is a form of faith, is relatively harmless as long as all it does is deceive the scientist into pushing his method too far. It is a very dangerous thing from a philosophic standpoint, however. It narrows the frame of reference. When a reductionist scheme fails because it has failed to take into account phenomena such as gravitational effects or color, what characteristically happens is that some property is attributed to the fundamental or lower-level entities that would not have been known except by studying their aggregate effects. For example, the only way we recognize gravitation is by examining an entire system. You could look at a single object all your life and not know it gravitates. Likewise, you could look at an electron all your life and not know anything about color. We discover certain kinds of properties only when they are evoked in the context of an aggregate or larger system.

Dr. Wilson, those who have read your classic work on human nature could easily suppose that you propose a reductionist scheme. You seem to argue that sociobiology, in principle, can explain anything, even ethical and religious beliefs. One of the strongest points in your presentation had to do with incest taboos. You took a relatively universal behavior common to a variety of religions and cultures and offered a genetic explanation for it. Yet, if one considers the diversity of cultures or the diversity of religions such as Islam and Christianity, it seems quite impossible to reduce their different value systems to something genetic. Since Christians and Moslems are not genetically diverse, one cannot explain their religious diversity genetically.

It makes sense to me to push sociobiology as a methodology as hard as you can. You will get some very nice things out of it. At the same time, if you make a more substantive claim. . . . But, perhaps you have moved from the stance you took on this matter in the 1970s.

Dr. Sperry's approach to consciousness is reminiscent of Michael Polanyi's. In *Personal Knowledge* and other works in the 1950s and 1960s, Polanyi constructed a hierarchical account of the natural world in terms of levels of activity culminating in consciousness. Polanyi, a very distinguished physical chemist turned philosopher, developed the notion of downward as well as upward causation. His attempt to work it out is worthy of attention, though not altogether satisfactory.

As I read Dr. Sperry's paper, his contribution to the broader discussion of religion and science can be taken either in a weaker or a stronger sense. The weaker sense is the assertion that your work has broken down an older form of determinism and reductionism that seemed incompatible with religious views. But, there is a stronger claim implicit in what Dr. Sperry is saying. If scientific and religious views are to be fused, and if the evidence of religion has got to be acceptable to the scientist, then God, insofar as he can appear in the natural system at all, is simply the upper state of that system. This is an entirely immanentist or pantheist view. Viewed from this perspective, your contribution to the cause of religion is that you have made that kind of God more plausible. You note in your paper that the separation of creation and creator must be ruled out. This is an important restriction from the theological standpoint. The notion of God that you are proposing is that of a higher level within nature itself.

DR. SPERRY: Let me begin with your last item, Fr. McMullin. I would think that in the eyes of science the creator or creative force system must exist at all levels. It is an evolving, hierarchic, multiform, multicomplex, multinested, much more sophisticated entity than the usual image would imply. But, the new outlook does give primacy to the higher over the lower level controls.

You are right that Polanyi expressed very similar ideas, as did Lloyd Morgan and Jan Smuts before him and W. E. Ritter before them. These emergent views go way back, but their status up through the early 1960s remained that of scattered, individual, occasional, minority philosophy. This is why I emphasized that I am speaking today not from the position of personal philosophy but from that of mainstream psychology. For the first time, a whole scientific discipline has espoused this sort of outlook. It is interesting to speculate what caused this change from relatively obscure minority philosophy to the dominant practicing paradigm of the behavioral sciences.

I believe that behavioral science, though as yet unaware of it, is leading the way toward a more valid paradigm for all science. I see in this no quarrel with microdeterminism as such, and, of course, everyone agrees that reductionism is still fine as methodology. When you come, however, to interpretations, to the building of world views, to deriving moral values, then the macrodeterminist principles have to be taken into account. They do not replace but supplement and/or complement microdeterminism and reductionism.

DR. WILSON: Fr. McMullin is right in saying that in the 1970s, when I was trying to develop a sense of where sociobiology would go, I was very optimistic in my writings about the possibility of a total reductionistic explanation of all phenomena. But, I never

meant those statements to be anything more than programmatic;
I was not proposing an absolute belief system. The spirit of science
is to press one's theory as far as possible. An astrophysicist once
put it beautifully when he said, "Let us see how high we can fly
before the sun melts the wax in our wings."

As to variation among cultures and religions, I believe sociobiology can cope with it. Even when there is a uniform genotype,
as is naturally the case in dealing with human behavior, mixed
strategies are possible—and indeed these have been explored in
the case of religious behavior. There can also be randomly generated
variation out of a single genotype of responses, a so-called norm of
reaction. Charles Lumsden and I treated some of these issues in
Promethean Fire. I grant that the air gets a bit thin and some of the
wax begins to melt at this level, but we are going to keep on trying.

FAITH AND SCIENCE

PRESIDER
Most Rev. A. James Quinn
Auxiliary Bishop of Cleveland

SPEAKER
Dr. Jerome J. Lejeune
Executive Director
Institut de Progenese (Paris)

RESPONDENT
Rev. Benedict Ashley, OP
Emeritus Professor
Aquinas Institute (St. Louis)

DISCUSSION

Dr. Jerome J. Lejeune

Pascal once said: *"Ce que les hommes par leurs plus grandes lumieres avaient pu connaitre, cette religion l'enseignait a ses enfants."* ("Religion teaches children what the human race has been able to learn only by the greatest intellectual effort.")

Faith and science express the truth, but their voices are very different. Faith, bestowed by grace, uses a poetic language the heart receives with joy. Science, laboriously earned, offers an abstract discourse the reason masters with pain. It is no wonder that these two paths to knowledge seem at one time mutually reinforcing, at another time in tension, according to the state of our understanding.

CONCORDISM

When clear divergences came to the fore with the explosive development of physical and biological theories, eminent minds tried to establish a precarious truce through resort to concordism. But, attempting to soften the hard outlines of science or to belittle the heights of revelation led only to repeated failure. In the great days of Laplacian determinism, for example, it was embarrassing to see the sun and the moon appearing on the fourth day. Some concordists argued that an earthbound observer could not see the lights of heaven until the clouds cleared. This is overingenious, to say the least. The state of knowledge in those days did not permit the idea that light could have existed before the sun came to be!

Another example. In the glory days of triumphant neo-Darwinism some ten to twenty years ago, the interpretation of Genesis was changed. Adam could no longer be thought of as an individual. The name, rather, was a generic term referring to a developing race of would-be humans. At this time, biologists believed that whole populations insensibly evolved by gradual steps into a new species over eons of time!

DISCORDISM

Concordism was progressively replaced by discordism. It became fashionable to see man as an anomaly fortuitously issued from an impassive universe. Our destiny, our duty are nowhere written; we remain forever incomprehensible.

This assertion is the "nul" hypothesis, a useful starting point that makes no assumptions not tied to observation. Observation will tell if the hypothesis must be rejected because it fails to fit available data. Only then can we construct more elaborate theories about humanity.

In the hands of some theorists, however, the hypothesis becomes a proscription. In the name of the postulate of objectivity so dear to Jacques Monod, they decree that no explanation in teleological terms will ever be acceptable. The universe, by definition, has no purpose and is leading nowhere. In a word, they want that God should not exist. It is the *discordism of pride*.

A strong reaction to so extreme a view is emerging, especially in the United States. Science knows almost nothing, say the creationists. (This, alas, is almost true, but not quite.) Therefore, Scripure must be taken literally; the creationists even add a bit to it. To avoid contradictions, they challenge all the inconvenient facts in advance. They do not want to grant science its legitimate rights. This attitude I call the *discordism of despair*.

Third and most dangerous, believers tend to withdraw. Fearing open discussion, they steer into "safe" waters. They conceal some revealed truth, hoping to preserve acceptance of what remains. Some catechisms start with Abraham, for example, in order to avoid dealing with Adam. This is the *discordism of cleverness*. It is not very charitable because it deprives us of parts of the message of life.

It is urgent that we examine the tension between religion and science with our cards on the table. Is there or is there not an irreducible contradiction between revealed teaching and the observed facts?

THE BEGINNING OF TIME

Let us glance at the first day of Genesis. God said, *"Fiat lux"* and the light was. Many years ago, Fr. Georges Lemaitre, illustrious president of the Pontifical Academy of Sciences, very aptly drew the conclusion to which the recession of the galaxies led. Hubble had shown that the faster a galaxy is receding, the farther away it is. The universe is a puff of dust blooming in the infinite; that is the meaning of the red shift. Fr. Lemaitre realized that, if this expansion had occurred over a long span of time, the universe was once contained in a smaller volume. At the beginning of time, there was only the primeval hyperdense speck, the source of all matter and energy.

The discordism of pride revolted against this notion of origin. It was too close to the notion of creation. (Recall that in the ancient world the universe was considered eternal. Only Jews and Christians supposed that it had begun.) The tumult died away over the years, since no other hypothesis can account for the facts. In the 1960s, radio astronomers discovered the three-Kelvin backgound radiation, the "echo" of the tremendous event marking the start of space and time. Scientists now generally concede that the universe had a definite beginning some twelve to fifteen billion years ago.

The primeval energy appeared as light; *"Fiat lux"* is the foundation of modern cosmology. Modestly, we now speak of the "big bang," not the "creation." It is good that physicists do not use the language of theology when they can express the same idea with a noncommittal phrase. Neither concordism nor discordism are relevant any longer; both are obsolete.

As Leibniz foresaw, the models of possible universes are infinite in number, and theorists continue to refine their concepts of the results of such a great and sudden surge of energy as the big bang. It is dangerous, though, to play fast and loose with the basic laws of nature in creating such models, whether the subject is interstellar gravity or the quantum mechanical behavior of atoms. If one assumes much divergence from the observed value of basic parameters, suddenly stars and planets become impossible. The physicochemical laws that allow living beings to utilize energy in order to live no longer apply. And, finally, one arrives at the conclusion that very few models allow for the existence of those who construct the models!

This does not imply, as Engels supposed, that matter is pregnant with spirit so that spirit will inevitably appear in some corner of the universe. It simply means that the laws of nature must be such as not to preclude our existence. This anthropic principle, defined by Brandon Carter, was expressed centuries ago by the sculptor of the portal of Chartres Cathedral, whose scene shows God creating the universe with Adam in mind. Once again, however, physicists are modest. They simply say that we must take human existence into account in examining the laws of the universe. Their logic is irrefutable.

THE FORMS OF LIFE

Let us consider evolution. Two creative acts frame the Genesis account: the creation of the universe at the beginning and the creation of humanity at the end. In between, God says, "Let the earth bring forth vegetation . . ." (Gn 1:11) and here are the plants; "Let the water teem with an abundance of living creatures, and on the earth let birds fly . . ." (Gn 1:20) and here are fish and later birds; "Let the earth bring forth all kinds of living creatures . . ." (Gn 1:24) and here are the animals; and man appears at the end. This dazzling summary tells us the same story, and in the same order, as is registered in those immense cemeteries of geological strata laid down over the ages. How the biblical authors got access to such knowledge science does not know.

Here, the discordism of despair is of no value. No explanatory hypothesis can contradict the biblical text, which does not tell us how the various species appeared. Creationism makes the error of adding an element to the biblical account, that is, the fixity of species. Each species must have been created as such, they say. Therefore, evolution is wrong.

There *is* a difficulty here, but it does not arise from the Bible, which outlines the steps of evolution. It arises from genetics and paleontology, which show species remaining unchanged for millions (insects) or even billions (bacteria) of years. Hence, the harshness of the controversies raging among theoreticians; reconciling the remarkable stability of species with the successive appearance of various forms of life is far from easy.

NEO-DARWINISM

Since species stagnate and life evolves, as Bergson said, there must be a way to pass from one species to another. Darwin supposed that the most convenient way to do so would be through the progressive accumulation of extremely small changes. If small variations occur by random change, the environment will sort them out. Climate, food supply, predators, and other factors will ensure that favorable mutations are transmitted to progeny, while the unfavorable are not. In a very stable environment, species will tend to remain stable, while rapid environmental change will promote the appearance of new forms. Thus, both the stability of species and evolution find an explanation. (Kimura notes that some neutral mutations are not selected either for or against. This adds some fancy to the picture, but the basic argument is unaffected.)

To put it succinctly, neo-Darwinian theory states that mutations are the motor and natural selection guide of biological evolution. Because mutations are random, and their effects are not determined by the environment to which creatures have to adapt, we are led to the blunt proposition that Monod borrowed from Democritus: "Everything in nature is the fruit of chance and of necessity." Such a system requires enormous trial and error, but geological periods are very long indeed. Neo-Darwinists have to believe that, given a long enough stretch of time, blind chance will produce the eye.

AN EXPERIMENT IN DETROIT

Aside from a few holdovers from Lysenkoism, no one today pretends to have witnessed a new species emerging from a parent one. While we may lack experimental evidence on living systems, however, a very interesting equivalent can be fruitfully studied, thanks to human ingenuity: the neo-Darwinian theory of automobile evolution!

From a biological point of view, an auto factory is very similar to a reproductive organ. All the cars from a given production line—perhaps we should call them a species—are quite identical but for some minor characteristics such as paint color (skin color for human beings). Every part is precisely made in conformity with detailed instructions stored on the magnetic tapes of the factory's computers, like the genetic information encoded in the DNA in our chromosomes.

All the human genetic machinery has a more or less close parallel in the car-manufacturing process. The parallel to natural selection is obvious. Every novelty introduced into the car will be judged by the consumer. If the "mutation" is superior to the older model, if it performs better, if it is better adapted to the marketplace environment, it becomes a hot-selling item. The factory will reproduce the selected mutation at an accelerated rate, and soon it will replace the old model entirely. It does not matter whether the selective advantage derives from a morphological change—the shape of the fenders—or a metabolic one—miles per gallon. What makes and measures success in the automobile business is the fitness of machine to environment, which determines the number of exemplars produced.

Given this set of facts, a neo-Darwinian bookkeeper at a car company might very logically say: "The whole of automobile evolution can be explained by sudden variations, appearing by chance and selected for and against by market conditions." He would be partly right if technological considerations are overlooked. The president of the company, however, would not be so naive. Suppose we offer a winning formula: "From time to time you just make a random change in your model. If the new model sells well, promote it; if not, junk it. Play this blind game long enough, and you will some day produce everyone's dream car. You may be absolutely certain of success. Nature herself has followed this path since it produced the first amoeba and look, here we are!"

The carmaker, thinking over our proposition, would realize that the more highly elaborated a system, the less likely that a random change will improve it. (Try randomly interchanging two connections on your personal computer and judge the results.) It follows that after each improvement the time required to achieve the next increases exponentially. No banker would underwrite such a random mutation/natural selection system. The time required to produce the dream car would be immeasurably greater than geological time. In real life, "money is time."

The carmaker would no doubt reject our system and instead consult an engineer regarding model changes. The car's previous evolution, after all, was guided by the engineer's discoveries. But we, alas, when faced with biological evolution, have no such option.

The mutations we know are random and no one knows of an engineer.

THE INGENUITY OF LIFE

Perhaps, the engineer is life itself? A few years ago, such a statement would have been considered absurd. Today, we know that complex organisms do not read their genetic message as bacteria do, stumbling letter by letter one step at a time. Complex organisms act like a film editor. After the cameramen produce miles of film, someone takes scissors to it, removing the useless passages and bringing together sequences that throw light on one another by complementarity or contrast.

While we have begun to recognize this work of recomposition, we do not understand why it is characteristic of complex organisms and not of bacteria. An extraordinary evolutionary jump remains unexplained. It is possible that an enormous gap exists in our knowledge.

METAMORPHOSIS

The neo-Darwinian story has it that one day a fish with reinforced fins hauled itself painfully ashore and conquered the continents. With the slow improvement of legs over the millenia, this fish's descendents became four-legged animals.

The summary seems plausible, but what about the mechanism involved? Let's consider a frog egg. A tadpole hatches from it. With its gills, its fins, its lateral sensitive line, this tadpole is in every respect physiologically and anatomically a fish. And, yet, one day, without mutation or selection, it loses his tail, grows legs, invents lungs, and becomes a tetrapod. This happens not over millions of years but before our eyes in a fish bowl! Apparently, our tadpole first found in its genes the code for a fish. Then, after a twist that thyroid hormone can trigger, it feverishly reread its genetic blueprint and executed the instructions to make a tetrapod. This tadpole knows more than we do.

And what about cellular differentiation, building bones, muscle, blood, and even brain—the most sophisticated computer ever conceived on earth—all coming out of the single fertilized egg? We are still completely ignorant of the mechanism that drives differentiation, as basic as it is to building up the organism, just as we are ignorant of the mechanism of metamorphosis. How futile it is to pretend we know how an elephant evolved from a primitive mouse, when we still do not understand how a tadpole becomes a frog.

SPECIES AND CHROMOSOMES

The order in which instructions are carried out is obviously very important. The DNA molecules that carry genetic instructions do not float in the juice of the cell like noodles in a bowl of soup. Not only are they located on the chromosome in a certain order typical of the species, but the chromosomes themselves have a length, number, and banding pattern absolutely characteristic of a given species.

The horse and donkey will serve to illustrate this reality. They are two different species because their hybrid, the mule, is sterile. Although better endowed for endurance and agility than its parents, the mule cannot procreate. The structural differences between the chromosomes of mare and ass are so great that no equilibrated repartition can be achieved during the maturation of the reproductive cells.

This genetic barrier, due to chromosomes and not mutation, is the very definition of the frontier between species. The sterility of hybrids means that a chromosomal novelty is inevitably selected against. Only when the novelty is received from both parents will fertility reappear, hence, the need for any chromosomal evolution to reach this homozygous stage as quickly as possible if speciation is to occur.

This need is best filled if the first creature homozygous for the novelty reproduces with itself by autofecundation. Such reproduction is quite feasible with plants; all the new species we have developed have been manufactured this way. In higher animals, the separation of the sexes forbids autofecundation. At this level, then, the need is best filled by generating the required couple all at once. Pathology offers an indication of how this might happen.

Extremely rarely, a male zygote, carrier of forty-six chromosomes, including one X and one Y, splits into twins. One of the twins continues its male identity. The other, not having received the Y chromosome, becomes an imperfect female with forty-five chromosomes, including only one X. (Normal females have two X chromosomes.) In my experience, a young girl thus affected complained that she could not look at herself in a mirror because she was afraid of seeing her brother. She was feeling a biological truth of which she was consciously unaware: she was really a fragment of the brother from whom she came.

In our species, "45,X" females are generally sterile (though some have produced children) but, in mice, they are perfectly fertile. The experiment remains to be done, but if a zygote of the type I have described was homozygous for a chromosomal novelty, the couple that developed from it, if mated, would originate a new species of mice.

I apologize for this long excursion into genetic engineering. The hypothesis I set forth would look very revolutionary and very modern and would be considered *the* solution to rapid evolutionary change if the story of Adam and Eve had not already been so much advertised! Science is very reluctant to discover truths already known for thousands of years.

PRIMATES AND THE MAN LIKE US

Two or three million years ago, an extraordinary flowering occurred in a vast zone ranging from Kenya through Palestine to Asia. New forms appeared rapidly: *homo habilis* and then *homo erectus*, whose brain case is larger than that of the modern apes. The causes of these developments are mysterious, but they give the impression of preparations for an important happening.

Some time between one hundred thousand and forty thousand years ago, the man like us, our own kind, suddenly appears. We are really newcomers. As far as is presently known, both Cro-Magnon and Neanderthal belong to our species. As I noted above, Genesis uses the word *create* when speaking of our origin. Yahweh modeled a woman as companion to the man from the latter's own flesh. "[T]he man said: This one, at last, is bone of my bones and flesh of my flesh; This one shall be called 'woman,' for out of 'her man' this one has been taken" (Gn 2:23).

Here is a deep mystery. Genetics can demonstrate that the most narrow consanguinity is necessary for the emergence of a new species, even that a couple born of the same zygote is the optimal way to begin. But, the fact that a special intervention, a creative act absolutely apart from the rest of evolution, was necessary for the emergence of our species is pure revelation—but not a real surprise.

A CURIOUS PHENOMEMON

Man is a curious phenomenon. He stands erect, manufactures tools, and speaks. To some extent, one can even rely on what he says. Anterior forms, however, were bipedal one or two million years ago. The first chips of stone may date from the same era. Some endocranian impressions suggest that Broca and Wernicke zones were sufficiently developed to allow a primitive communication system even in *homo habilis*.

The full novelty, the absolute superiority, consists in the fact that man is the only creature able to experience a kind of connivance between the laws of nature and his feeling of existence. The faculty of admiration is solely human. No dog ever tasted the fragrance of a rose. No chimp ever contemplated the sunset or the splendor of the starry sky. The one who was the first to know he would die and built tombs; the one who helped wounded fellows and protected their weakness; the one who discovered art and pursued it far beyond mere technique; this one who is us—and not a hundred thousand years old—possesses something like a spark of the intelligent love.

Besides the difficulties it presents at delivery, man's large brain is an enigma of natural selection, as Alfred Russel Wallace was the first to recognize. Before we could develop our ability to decipher the laws of nature, leading to such achievements as unleashing the power of the atom and visiting the planets, generation after generation had to accumulate a fantastic store of knowledge. How could natural selection anticipate the need for this knowledge? That the world is intelligible, even partially, is perfectly unintelligible, unless the Spirit who enacted its laws also created us in his own image.

THE RIB, THE TREES, AND THE GARDEN

Let us glance again at the Genesis account. It refers to Adam's rib or, more precisely, pair of ribs. Why associate the birth of our species with the loss of these small bones? Modern exegetes embarrassed by this anatomical precision might be interested to know that our nearest cousins, the gorilla and the chimpanzee, have thirteen ribs to our twelve. There is no need to attempt building a new concordism on this circumstance. On the other hand, it is wise to transmit the whole message untouched for the sake of science's continued evolution. Theories fade away, but the truth is everlasting.

During discussion following a talk I recently gave on the origin of the human species, after I had described the "one-couple expedient" as suggested by genetics, a knowledgeable member of the audience called out: "Let us suppose you attained your bipedal being, naked, without fangs, without claws . . . and capable of admiration. How will you protect it from the first predator that comes along?"

"With your permission, sir," I replied, "I will place him in a carefully preserved park, an agreeable garden."

"And, will you take care that it does not pick up some toxic food that could unbalance its mind?"

I did not answer. A poison paralysing the connections between the affective network and the intellective one and capable, at the same time, of modifying the primitive genetic instructions that dictate the makeup of these parts of the brain. . . . I cannot describe such a poison in scientific terms. Yet, philosophers down through the ages have noted the existence of a primeval fault in our makeup. It consists of an inability to integrate the emotional and the logical. Most of the time, the heart and the head are not on speaking terms!

With this consideration, we are back to our starting point. Revelation speaks to the heart, experiment to reason. Can we ever integrate them? It has happened once.

A SIGN IN THE HEAVENS

Some two thousand years ago, a delegation of astronomers came to Jerusalem from the East. They had observed a moving sign in the sky that, according to their calculations, announced some sort of good news. They had derived the direction in which to search, but not the precise location.

The astronomers had an audience with the king, who immediately summoned his counselors. They did not understand the situation but sensed that there was something to fear; good news is not necessarily good to the establishment. To leave no stone un-turned, the king interrogated theologians. They revealed that a minor prophet had once written: "But you, Bethlehem-Ephrathah, too small to be among the clans of Judah, From you shall come forth for me one who is to be ruler in Israel; Whose origin is from of old, from ancient times" (Mi 5:1).

So, the Magi were to go to Bethlehem. They felt great joy when the sign in the sky stood still, confirming this advice. Thus, they made the most admirable discovery: the creature conceived in per-fection, having, by the action of the Spirit, given birth to the new Adam. They saw the Virgin and the Infant.

This story is marvelous not only because it is true but also because it points the way to a healthy relationship between science and faith. The Magi did not doubt the competence of the theologians. They decided to go and see.

For their part, the theologians did not raise their noses from the text. Perhaps, I am reading in here. Matthew is a charming sto-ryteller, however, and he would not have missed the chance to portray Herod, his court, and his experts craning their necks to catch a glimpse of what the Magi were admiring. I am sure they did no such thing. And, even had they gone, they would not have seen what the wise men saw. Great patience is needed to decipher nature.

Thus, teamwork led people of good will to the highest truth. Everyone conscientiously listened to the other without scanting his own hard-won knowledge. As for the political power, duly enlight-ened by faith and informed by science, it behaved as usual. Invoking reasons of state, it massacred the innocents.

THE CHILDREN OF MEN

Our own time is witnessing the same thing. All molecular biology teaches us that human nature is given at conception. The most recent technology, *in vitro* fertilization, demonstrates that a new being comes into existence at conception. The most sophisticated ultrasonic scanning shows us the two-month-old baby performing, in the mother's womb, a kind of dance, full of grace and youth. The Church teaches the same unchanging truth. Nevertheless, the political power has reversed by vote what doctors have sworn to for more than two thousand years: "I will not give poison; I will not procure abortion."

Then, one receives in the heart this terrible revelation transmitted by our Lord himself, this decree incomprehensible yet absolutely obvious. "I offer you praise, O Father, Lord of heaven and earth, because what you have hidden from the learned and the clever you have revealed to the merest children" (Lk 10:21).

Rev. Benedict Ashley, OP

Each of our speakers has tried to clarify the distinction between science and religion and their mutual relations. *Science* has been implicitly defined as the systematic investigation of empirical reality, chiefly by the observational and experimental testing of theoretical hypotheses. *Religion* has generally been taken to mean theism in its Christian and Catholic expression; the authoritative texts referred to have been the Bible and papal and conciliar documents.

All the speakers have agreed that science and religion are very different kinds of human activity, but they have not agreed on how the two are related. To adopt Dr. Lejeune's terms, perhaps we can classify these relations as concordism or discordism. Fr. McMullin, in his keynote address, and Dr. Wilson, in different ways, seemed to favor a discordant view. For Fr. McMullin, religion, unlike science, is not explanatory but salvational. Theology, while taking care not to propose views that science can disprove, should not expect from science any proof of its own positions because the hypothetical and transient character of the scientific method makes all such proofs unstable and undermines religious claims to certitude. Dr. Wilson, on the other hand, believes that religion is explanatory but suggests that its explanations will ultimately be replaced by those of science. Sociobiology will show that religion is rooted in human instincts necessary for survival—necessary not because religion explains reality but because it fosters hopeful attitudes and group solidarity by providing common symbols.

On the other hand, Dr. Dyson and Dr. Sperry favor a concordant view of the science-religion relation. Dr. Dyson presented us with an actual synthesis, a scientific-religious world view capable, he thinks, of accounting for both the order in the world and its rich diversity, even its incompleteness and tragedy. Finally, Dr. Sperry has assured us that the cognitive developments in psychology open the way to overcoming the discord between materialism and spiritual reality, which has made religion and science rivals in the manner posited by Dr. Wilson. What is noteworthy about Dr. Dyson's and Dr. Sperry's concordism is that both will only admit a God who, in Fr. McMullin's terms, is a "part of the world system," not a Creator absolutely distinct from the world and independent of it as is the God of the Bible and the Koran.

I have briefly reviewed these views because I think we need to keep them in mind if we are fully to appreciate what Dr. Lejeune has just said. He accepts the position that science and religion are very distinct types of knowledge. However, he relates them differently, attempting to avoid both concordism and discordism. As far as concordism is concerned, he fears not so much that religion will repeat its error of condemning Galileo by contradicting the findings of science as that it will be tempted to modify its eternal truths to conform them to the transitory hypotheses of science.

On the other hand, Dr. Lejeune warns against three kinds of discordism: (1) that of pride (Jacques Monod), which denies all purpose and meaning to the world in the name of science; (2) that of despair, typified by the creationists who reject modern science's attempts to explain the world and look to the Bible for true science; (3) that of cleverness, which, in the name of faith, avoids facing any of the apparent conflicts between the Bible and science.

The subtle and imaginative middle way that Dr. Lejeune has proposed, which he exemplifies by his own great achievements as an independent-minded and creative geneticist, is to allow religious and scientific thought to develop freely along their own lines without great worry about the apparent contradictions that inevitably arise from time to time. Science proceeds in a hypothetical way, sometimes with marked shifts, while religious truth claims to share in the constancy of God himself. This does not mean, according to Dr. Lejeune, that the relation between the Bible and science is simply one of noncontradiction. Rather, the two modes of understanding seem at times to contradict, at other times to confirm, one another. Thus, the discoveries of science help us to see ancient insights contained in the poetic biblical accounts, which we had not seen previously, while these biblical insights give a deeper human meaning to scientific discoveries that, of themselves, might seem to make our universe seem ever more alien and absurd.

Dr. Lejeune illustrated this thesis in a number of striking ways. The big-bang hypothesis may not demonstrate the existence of a Creator, but at least it shakes those who believe that science must presuppose a self-explanatory world. The anthropic principle may not be a scientific law, but at least it shows us that the laws of nature must remain within narrow parameters if they are not to preclude our existence. The Genesis account of the origin of species, in the creative word of God, points out to us that evolution involves not only the birth but also the relative stability and distinction of species. It also calls attention to the fact that neo-Darwinian evolution is not a final explanation of the origin and diversification of life, a matter that, in many ways, still remains mysterious. Even the account of the creation of woman from Adam's side and the placing of the original pair in the garden contains profound insights about the relation of the sexes and of humanity to its environment, insights that may suggest to the scientists certain interesting hypotheses.

Dr. Lejeune concluded his paper by interpreting another famous biblical account—this time from the New Testament and the prophet Micah—as a kind of parable that may help us to a better understanding of the relation between science and religion. He compares those ancient astrologers, the Magi, to scientists who, through their science (which may in the end prove as shaky as astrology but which requires vast patience and research), can come to worship Emmanuel, God with us. On the other hand, he compares theologians to the ancient biblical exegetes who pointed the way to the Magi, yet kept their eyes fixed on the sacred text of revelation. Thus, the two books of St. Augustine to which Fr. McMullin referred can mutually interpret each other. While science and religion go their own ways, from time to time, each can help the other correctly interpret its insights.

I find Dr. Lejeune's conception very attractive. Its advantages are that it recognizes that the religious and scientific modes of thought need not be rigidly yoked together in a strict concordance if they do not claim to be able to do more than they can. Thus, they will have creative freedom without seeking to destroy one another. On the other hand, their relation need not be merely negative and discordant but positive and mutually interpretative.

In my opinion, however, it is possible to retain this freedom and, at the same time, move toward a more continuous and articulated relationship between the Christian world view and the achievements of modern science. When we read the Bible, the effort to reconstruct the historical development of the biblical world view is indeed helpful and indispensable, but theologically and religiously, it is only secondary. Religious belief rests not on these historical reconstructions but on the completed canon of the Bible, which alone has the guarantee of inspiration.

Recent advances in canonical criticism show us that salvation history, as presented in the Bible, as a whole, cannot be understood except in the context of the Wisdom tradition in which Yahweh is known as Creator. Redemption or salvation is a restoration and completion of the original plan of creation. Moreover, the saving God who revealed himself in a special way to the Jews did so only after first revealing himself to all humankind in the creation. Consequently, Vatican I taught and Vatican II confirmed the teaching of the Wisdom literature and of St. Paul that God has made himself known to all through his creation. The Catholic faith is confident that God's existence can be known with certitude, even by non-believers from their experience of the visible and empirical world.

Christian philosophers have attempted to formulate such proofs of the existence of God critically and precisely (and, I think, successfully). When scientific theories, however temporally successful, seem to undermine such proofs, it behooves Christian philosophers and theologians either to clarify the proofs so as to remove apparent contradictions or to raise questions for the scientists about the solidity of their theories. To raise such questions to scientists is not censorship but a necessary part of honest dialogue. As Dr. Lejeune has indicated, we should not be alarmed at such conflicts of ideas, provided their significance is not exaggerated.

But, the real contribution of science to theology is not to demonstrate the existence of God; such demonstrations rest on general principles such as "matter constantly undergoes change" and "nothing happens without a proper cause." Rather, science can help fill out our understanding of who God is. The real problem with the notion of God as Prime Mover is that it is extremely abstract. To fill in that abstraction with rich content, necessary if we are to worship, love, and trust in God, it is necessary that we study his creation and its historical development in ever greater detail. According to Aristotle, the Divine Artist is known by studying the least details of his works. All of modern science, all the wonders of which we have been hearing, and countless more still to be discovered help us more and more to know what their Maker is like.

Of course, the Christian believes that the ultimate revelation of God is in Jesus Christ, who is God present in person in a way visible and tangible to us. But, Jesus himself remains a shadowy figure until we realize that whatever good we find in other human beings has its source in him. Consequently, to know Jesus Christ and, in him, to know God, we need to know what it is to be human in all its details, not merely of mind and soul but even of the body, which in the Resurrection is forever ours. That means that whatever science can tell us has religious value, including whatever it can tell us about the cosmos out of which we have emerged.

Religion must free itself from that dualism that would separate body and soul, the empirical and the transcendental, science and faith. It must actively encourage science in its researches, while leaving it the proper speculative freedom necessary for such research. Further, theology can motivate scientists and show them the value of their work by integrating it into a wider view of reality so that it participates in that wonder and praise of God that is prayer, the supreme life of humanity.

Discussion

BISHOP QUINN: Dr. Lejeune and Fr. Ashley have set the stage for a most interesting discussion, it seems to me. Who would like to lead off?

DR. DENNIS DOHERTY: With regard to Dr. Lejeune's comments on the use of noncommittal language, our group feels that scientists should explain things in terms proper to science. Let them speak their own language. We feel, too, that people of religious faith have a responsibility to interpret, in religious terms, what science talks about.

We have two questions for Dr. Lejeune. First, How do you view the recent works of Eldridge and Gould regarding the long-term stability of species? Second, What ought to be the goal of dialogue between religion and science? We found benefit in Fr. Ashley's response. Granted the stance of the believer, science can paint in the details.

DR. LEJEUNE: I would say that Eldridge and Gould improved upon previous knowledge that sometimes new species emerge very rapidly in geological terms. It is a very interesting discovery, but it does not change my views because I have never been a believer in strict neo-Darwinism. Gould's intervention is most agreeable to me because it seems to be true.

What should the goal of the dialogue be? I said at the beginning that religion speaks to the heart and science to the reason. Interest in the dialogue reflects the human dignity of putting together the feeling of the heart and the deductions of reason. That is what is called a state of grace.

DR. FREDERICK LAWRENCE: Our group was most impressed by Dr. Lejeune's genial reincarnation of the spirit of Pascal. When one is a serious scientist and, at the same time, a serious believer and allows the two things to illuminate each other, it is an impressive and wonderful thing, no matter how many difficulties emerge.

We also wonder about what you might call "the dynamics of high vulgarization," when scientists and religious leaders talk about their differences. I have heard scientists use Scripture in a way that could be labeled unprofessional. On the other hand, how scientists must squirm when theologians make pronouncements on matters where they are less than expert. How do we deal with this?

We made some observations on what happens when the two cultures of religion and science are combined in the same person. In most of our experience, the younger the person the greater schizophrenia there is between the religious and scientific aspects. Older people, on other hand, tend to be more "myth-loving," to try to bring everything together. We wondered how priest-scientists resolve these tensions.

More attention should be paid, we feel, to the discordances between religion and science, to the different character of the truth claims that each makes. Science operates on the presumption that its conclusions are merely probable, that they are open to revision. Catholic theology, in fact most Christian theology, claims that at least some of its statements are not open to revision. What happens to theology when it moves too far in science's direction? Doesn't it have to remain faithful to its foundations in religious belief? But, can it maintain intellectual probity without gravitating toward science?

Science has a responsibility to accommodate itself as well. Foundational issues arise in all the sciences. It belongs to the integrity of science to face these foundational issues, and this means interchange with philosophy, theology, and religion. What are the criteria of truth in these different universes of discourse? We need to define what we mean by *religion, faith,* and *science.*

DR. AVROM BLUMBERG: The question arose in our discussion as to whether scientists need to invoke creation to make sense of the world. Scientists are very frugal with models; we hate to go out on limbs. Also, whenever an explanation is given, it always leads to another question. So, we prefer to describe rather than to explain. The big-bang theory is an adequate model, but it doesn't at all explain what brought all that matter or energy together in the primeval spark.

Dr. Lejeune makes a point that also fascinated Einstein, namely, that there is no particular reason why the world should make sense. He puts it this way: "That the world is intelligible, even partially, is perfectly unintelligible, unless the Spirit who enacted its laws also created us in his own image." There may be an opening to fruitful discussion here. Scientists have faith that there is order and design in the universe. Historically, this notion came from the concept that there is a God, so, in a sense, belief in God gave rise both to religion and science.

Our group discussed, at length, the fact that theologians rarely have scientific backgrounds. A number of theologians have remarked that their seminary training did not include any course in science. It was also pointed out, however, that one year of science usually does no good because science is presented as a finished product; the student doesn't get a clear idea of how science shapes its models.

Finally, we wanted to ask Dr. Lejeune whether he is suggesting that the Genesis account of human creation is a fact.

DR. LEJEUNE: You want to know if I consider the creation a report of a historical phenomenon? I have no information on that score. I am interested in trying to discover, from what we know about cytogenetics (the mechanics of the chromosomes), the best model for building new species with the highest probability of getting a correct result. It appears, from the equations of population genetics, that a very tiny population is necessary as regards evolution at the human level. The closer the consanguinity, brother and sister mating perhaps, the greater the probability that a change will reach the homozygous stage and that a new species will be built from there. So, one is led to propose the couple born from a single egg as the starting point for the human race. Thus, I constructed my theory.

I did not attempt to prove this theory in my talk; I was merely discussing a possibility. Now, let's suppose that we have done the experiment I proposed, that we have done some genetic engineering and succeeded in building a new species of mice, recognizable as such and entirely sterile with respect to the original population. Let's suppose this is possible. Even this experiment would not *prove* that Adam and Eve are a historical fact. It would only demonstrate an interesting system for building a new species: taking the female out of the male. Did it happen that way in the particular case of humanity? God knows.

FR. MCMULLIN: I want to make an observation first and then ask a question. I was charmed by the Gallic eloquence of our speaker. He is in the great tradition not only of Pascal but of Teilhard de Chardin. I heard echoes of a long tradition of poetry and rhetoric as well as of great science.

I was a student of Fr. Lemaitre when Pope Pius XII gave his allocution to the Pontifical Academy of Sciences in 1951. I had Lemaitre in a seminar shortly after he came back from the Academy meeting, and he was upset at the way the pope had used his big-bang theory as almost a proof for the existence of God. I still remember one of his comments, which has turned out to be scientifically prophetic: "How does His Holiness know that the big bang wasn't preceded by a big squeeze?" As we all know, the cyclical universe is now considered a possibility.

Lemaitre would have been perfectly happy to acknowledge a broad resonance between religious and scientific opinion in this matter. He would have agreed that, if God created the universe at a moment in time, that moment must have looked something like a big bang. But, that was as far as he would be willing to go in the way of argument.

Fred Hoyle, by the way, was also upset by that allocution and deliberately used the term *creation* for his own opposing theory, the "continuous creation" view. (His coworkers called it the "steady state theory.") That particular view went down in the 1960s, of course, because of the discovery of the three-Kelvin radiation.

I have a question regarding something I find troubling in your talk, Dr. Lejeune. I want to press you a little on this, just as I would have pressed Bergson or Teilhard, because I catch echoes in your thought of theirs. The question is prompted, in part, by your choice of the "Detroit analogy." As you pointed out, engineers are in charge of these automotive "mutations." So, they aren't random mutations.

Most people in evolutionary biology today, I think, would agree that the neo-Darwinian synthesis is not a final account, that it doesn't explain everything. Most would say neo-Darwinism has correctly outlined the process and identified the proper explanatory resources, though some additions may be needed. You proposed an extremely interesting conjecture regarding the origin of species. Should we take your suggestion as yet another in a long line of amendments to the neo-Darwinian synthesis? Or, are you suggesting, since you criticize the notion of chance, that somehow evolutionary events are not chance—that there is an *elan vital* or psychic energy moving through the process? How are we to construe the notion of chance in the light of your remarks?

DR. LEJEUNE: That is not easy to answer. First, let me say that, while I like the writings of Fred Hoyle, he was wrong to use the term *creation* in describing his steady state cosmology. If his model is true, nothing is created.

FR. MCMULLIN: According to him, one atom of hydrogen was created every million years or so per cubic yard of space.

DR. LEJEUNE: But, it was not created out of nothing. It was created out of a "special property of the void."

You asked about my criticisms of neo-Darwinism. First, what I propose about chromosomal mechanics does not come out of the blue. We know that each species has its own chromosomal makeup. That must mean something; we cannot ignore the fact. Yet, it has been entirely ignored in books about evolution. Second, you will never find an entry for *metamorphosis* in the index of a neo-Darwinian book. This suggests to me that those who write these scholarly books about evolution, about neo-Darwinian theory, have deliberately overlooked the fact that there are many ways of looking at the same genetic makeup. A tadpole does a fantastic job of climbing the taxonomic tree in fifteen days' time.

I suspect that behind the chromosomal mechanism there lie special phenomena of living systems that will entirely change our view of evolution. If you want to press me to the limit, I can tell you what I feel. It is just a feeling, an imagination, an opinion, not a scientific demonstration. I believe that the genes in the chromosomes are disposed in such a way that the genetic message, during the life of the cell, is expressed three-dimensionally. Generally, we think of this message as written on a linear molecule so that it is a linear system, like a magnetic tape. But, I suspect it is not like that in the living cell.

My hypothesis is that, with the specialization of the cell—whether it becomes a brain cell, an epidermic cell, or an hepatic cell—a particular way of reading this message develops. For example, segment A of a given chromosome is placed in proximity to gene B of another chromosome so that A and B can be read in order or so that A can act on B, turning it on or off.

Step by step, these chromosomes will constitute a three-dimensional design, very comparable to the logical network of a computer—the wiring being specific to a given tissue or organ at a given moment of the development of the individual from the egg state to the completed adult. Time, so to speak, is progressively incorporated in this progressive network.

So much for specialization of cells. Let's look at evolution. Let's suppose that an accident, a chromosomal mutation, occurs so that genes A and B, which only came in contact after quite an elaborate process of cell differentiation, are now definitely joined in a rearranged chromosome. If this accident happens in a reproductive cell, it will give to the next generation logical information built in the linear order of the new chromosome; a fantastic acceleration of the developmental process!

This chromosomal novelty should not be considered purely random; first, because it happened between two points that had already been placed in proximity by a physiological process; and, second, because it encodes in the linear message an information that was previously expressed in the three-dimensional construction. If such a novelty establishes itself in the homozygous state, it will modify the resulting network, hence the physiology.

One can then suppose that the next chromosomal change to occur in this lineage will have some causal relationship with the previous one. In other words, a given line will obstinately move in its own particular direction. The ancestors of horses try to become more and more horse-like, not cow-like.

Certainly, these very simple and rough ideas do not pretend to represent a new theory of evolutionary forces. But, my strong feeling—you asked for it—is that some day we will better understand these processes and discover some logic underlying apparently random accidents. The neo-Darwinian model does not provide this logic. Nevertheless, it *must* exist.

To illustrate: a chromosomal rearrangement in a cancer cell may place gene A (an oncogene) into proximity with gene B. The behavior of the cell changes as a result and, depending upon the chromosome involved, a leukemia of such and such a type, perfectly recognizable, is produced. Hence, the hypothesis that chromosomal changes can modify the makeup of an organism (and, if established, produce a new species) is not pure fancy. It is just an extrapolation of what we have learned in the last five years about the evolution of cancer cells.

It is futile to pretend to the public that we understand how an amoeba evolved into a man, when we cannot tell our students how a human egg produces a skin cell or a brain cell! The very broad field of research I have outlined may give us some hints about both phenomena. It is hoped that it will give us new and better ideas.

FR. ASHLEY: You mentioned that species can be recognized on the cellular level by chromosomal number and shape. We also know that the human species includes people with forty-seven chromosomes—for example, those with trisomy 21. If you tried to define the human species in terms of forty-six chromosomes—the "normal" number—you would have trouble with the person who has forty-seven. Somehow, the definition has to take this reality into account. My first question is this: Would the definition of species be more complete if it included chromosomal banding?

My second question also has to do with species. In zoology, an individual is said to belong to a certain species when it can only breed with members of that species. Is fertility the only external test we have to determine species? What constitutes a really new species in the sense in which you are using the term?

DR. LEJEUNE: I accept the Aristotelian notion of species: the members of one species can crossbreed and their progeny is fertile. Also, it can be said that individuals who crossbreed are more similar than others who cannot. That is true and is the taxonomic definition, but the species identity is related to its karyotype, the shape of its chromosomes. Indeed, banding pattern helps greatly in recognizing the fact that each species has its own peculiar karyotype.

You ask me whether I should say that a Down's syndrome baby is not a member of our species because he has forty-seven chromosomes instead of forty-six. Well, he has one chromosome too many—three exemplars of pair 21—but, the other forty-six chromosomes are typically human, not chimpanzee-like or orangutan-like or gorilla-like. Hence, I see him first as a man, second as a patient with a disease—trisomy 21. If this patient later procreates, fertility will be observed.

On the contrary, if two individuals differ by their specific karyotype, rather than by a simple error as in Down's Syndrome, we can safely predict that hybrids, if possible at all, will be sterile, as in the case of horse and ass. This explains why I use a chromosomal and genealogical definition of the term *species*. I realize that some people are using *species* more loosely, in ways that seem to me scientifically unuseful. I will go a little further and say that I have a deep respect for Darwin, but not his use of English. If he had called his book *The Origin of Races*, I would be a Darwinian. Unfortunately, he called it *The Origin of Species*, and I cannot accept it.

DR. WILSON: This is fun because it is beginning to turn into a lively scientific debate. I don't want to take too much time, but I felt I must say that I recognize very little of modern biology in what Dr. Lejeune is saying. I find the model that he is presenting, insofar as I understand it, singularly unconvincing and without a shred of evidence. It seems an attempt to revive orthogenesis at the molecular level. It should also be noted that his view is surely shared by less than one percent of the biologists of the world or, at least, the Western world. I myself know of no active evolutionary biologist in the United States or Great Britain who shares such a view.

I realize discovery lies in recognizing that all great oaks from small acorns grow. Today's heresy may well be tomorrow's orthodoxy. Nevertheless, Dr. Lejeune, the definition of species you have given is shared by scarcely any modern evolutionary biologists.

DR. LEJEUNE: I know.

DR. WILSON: A species is defined almost universally now—and it has become very effective as an operational definition—as "a population or series of populations isolated reproductively from other populations under natural conditions." It has been demonstrated in many animal species, particularly insects, that a single gene difference or a very small number of polygenes can quickly produce species. Take this case, for example: a biological species is reproductively isolated from another. Fertility is not required because premating isolating mechanisms—that is, ones that stop any attempt to mate prior to the actual formation of the fertilized egg—can be and demonstrably are equally effective. Molecular changes in a single sex pheromone, for example, have been sufficient to create species.

I was dismayed earlier by your analogy with the factory process. Whereas the manager of a Ford assembly plant would definitely be unwilling to stake the business on the success of a modification in the fender, this does not reflect the situation in nature, where profligate discard of parts is routine. There are between one billion billion and one hundred billion billion organisms alive at any given time on the earth's surface, many of which have life spans of only a few hours. Each one of these, depending on the organism, has between one thousand and ten billion nucleotide pairs. Thus, the arena of evolution by natural selection is almost unimaginably large. Nature's prodigious discard of nonworking parts has resulted in the extinction of more than ninety-nine percent of the species lines that have ever existed. Most biologists, and not just neo-Darwinians, see this process as adequate for explaining a large part of evolution.

You expressed puzzlement over the role of metamorphosis—the transformation of tadpole into frog. This is no mystery at all. Metamorphosis is easily fitted within the neo-Darwinian scheme. The relevant genotype evolved over a long period of time. This genotype includes multiple sets of genes so organized that the activation of one gene set produces one phenotype and the activation of another gene set produces another. Molecular genetics can explain this mechanism quite well. I must rise heartily to the defense of neo-Darwinian theory. The group will find me substantially more dogmatic and inflexible in this case than I was in the face of God.

DR. LEJEUNE: You say that only one percent of the geneticists now living are dissatisfied with neo-Darwinism. Does this mean that less than one percent will eventually accept a chromosomal hypothesis?

DR. WILSON: No, I meant that less than one percent of active biologists would agree with your dismissal of neo-Darwinism. That is totally different from saying that neo-Darwinism has fully explained everything. It is a non sequitur to argue on the basis of large gaps in our understanding of developmental biology and the speciation process that neo-Darwinism is bankrupt and must be replaced with another orthogenetic theory.

DR. LEJEUNE: In that case, I fully agree that less than one percent of the world's biologists would accept a new theory of evolution through chromosomes. It is a pity. I say that in all seriousness. In the face of evidence derived from all species that the chromosomal structure is so intimately involved in the speciation process, how can you construct an evolutionary theory that does not take this basic phenomenon into account?

DR. WILSON: I think there must be some misunderstanding. The role of cytogenetics and chromosome mechanics as primary processes in evolution, and in fact as part of the phenotype of evolution, is well worked out and integrated into neo-Darwinian theory. I don't follow your argument that they have been neglected.

DR. LEJEUNE: The notion that chromosomal change is what is important in evolution has significant implications. Chromosomal change will be selected against as soon as it occurs. On the contrary, if a small mutation has even a tiny selective advantage, it can grow in the population and be accumulated. That is one basic difference between the two explanations. The second difference is that we have strong reason to believe that chromosomal changes are not random, while most mutations do appear to be random. Obviously, we are dealing with two distinct ways of building an explanatory model.

DR. JAMES COURTRIGHT: The gaps that have been talked about are, in fact, being closed. I know of many instances in the last few years of recombinant procedures where genes have been replaced in mammalian and other cells. Genes, by themselves, can be put back into systems and expressed in a very specific way so that the gene itself is responsible for its expression in a given tissue at a given time. Moreover, we now know that enormous numbers of mobile genetic elements are present in eukaryotic chromosomes and that they are responsible for changes in these chromosomes. These discoveries are relevant to the questions Dr. Lejeune has been raising. A great deal of molecular information exists that allows us to understand evolutionary mechanisms in the neo-Darwinian context.

PARTICIPANT: I think the gaps in neo-Darwinism's ability to explain evolutionary change are there, perhaps even more radically than Dr. Wilson was acknowledging. I am not clear, however, where you are taking this point, Dr. Lejeune. Are you saying that these gaps will be filled by more complete scientific analysis of the chromosome structure? Or that a more wholistic view of the interaction of the total organism with the chromosome is required? Or that, in the last analysis, chromosomal changes are not random but are controlled by God or by some other force? Would you care to comment on the religious significance of the gaps?

DR. LEJEUNE: I do not find any religious significance in these gaps. I do assert that we do not take chromosomal mechanics and chromosomal physiology sufficiently into account in explaining evolution. And, we are wrong. We will do so sooner or later.

I don't know how long it will take before we can produce a more refined model than neo-Darwinism. In my view, neo-Darwinism is like the epicycles of Ptolemy: an explanation useful for the time it was proposed, but which did not exhaust the reality. In due course, Ptolemy's system gave way to the Copernician system, a better explanation. I think we are in the same place as regards evolution. Neo-Darwinism is a marvelous mathematical construct, as the epicycles of Ptolemy were. But even Ptolemy himself knew his calculations did not entirely fit. In the same way, we know that neo-Darwinism, as it is taught in the universities, does not give us a really satisfactory explanation, and we know further that there is one branch of science that is not incorporated in the theory. Obviously, somebody someday will produce a much better system. He will be evolution's Copernicus.

My interest in those gaps does not arise because I would like to squeeze in divine action. I do not believe that God manifests himself only where science fails! The fact that science exists at all is to me

a clear manifestation of God. But, our theories are far from satisfactory, and we must fill the gaps with more and better science.

Now, there is one idea to which I am very open, however. Man
is a very extraordinary anomaly compared with the rest of the living
kingdom. It would not surprise me, as a scientist, if a touch of
genius went into designing him.

THE RELATIONSHIP
BETWEEN SCIENCE AND RELIGION

PRESIDER
Most Rev. Dale J. Melczek
Auxiliary Bishop of Detroit

SPEAKER
Dr. Ian G. Barbour
Professor of Religion
Carleton College

DISCUSSION

Dr. Ian G. Barbour

SCIENCE AND RELIGION IN CONFLICT

There are two versions of the view that science and religion are in conflict. One is a critique of science in the name of religion, and the other is a critique of religion in the name of science.

Biblical Literalism: A Challenge to Science

Since the rise of modern science, there have been religious leaders who have rejected particular scientific theories as inconsistent with a literal interpretation of Scripture. But, in the past two decades, a new movement called "scientific creationism" has arisen that asserts that scientific evidence exists for the creation of the world within the last few thousand years. Its proponents want "creationist theory" to have equal time with evolutionary theory in high school biology texts and classes. The U.S. District Court in Arkansas rejected the claim that "scientific creationism" is science. It was shown that scientific creationists have not submitted research papers to scientific journals. They are clearly a religious group with a particular view of scriptural interpretation, and the separation of church and state forbids the teaching of one particular set of religious views in public schools.

No one at this conference has defended biblical literalism. The Catholic Church has been able to avoid this particular conflict because of its traditional acknowledgment of a variety of literary forms in Scripture. The first chapter of Genesis can be seen as a symbolic assertion of the world's goodness, orderliness, and dependence on God, rather than as a literal account of historical events. Fr. McMullin indicated that as early as Augustine the seven days were interpreted metaphorically. Protestants are more divided. Fundamentalists and some evangelical groups see Scripture itself as the direct channel of divine revelation. But, most mainline denominations hold that revelation occurred in the lives of the prophets and apostles and, above all, in the life and person of Christ, with Scripture as the human interpretation of these events. "Scientific creationism" is thus subject to criticism on religious grounds as much as on scientific grounds.

Now, Dr. Lejeune is a long way from the "scientific creationists." He is a very distinguished scientist. He clearly accepts a long period of evolution, so, presumably, he takes the seven days of the first chapter of Genesis symbolically. But, I wonder if there isn't a literalism in his reading of Genesis 2. Many Protestants interpret Adam purely symbolically: Adam is Everyman; Adam is each of us in our movement from innocence to disobedience to guilt; Adam is an image of fallen human nature. I know that Catholic thought insists on Adam and Eve as a unique historical couple, but it has always been my understanding that this is seen as a requirement of the theological doctrine of original sin and not as the product of a literal reading of Scripture. One could defend the existence of a unique couple without trying to justify the details of Adam's missing ribs or, showing, as Dr. Lejeune did at some length, how Adam and Eve could have developed from the same fertilized egg. Is there an echo of concordism here in the attempt to give scientific explanations for literally interpreted scriptural passages? If one can accept the details of the first chapter of Genesis as symbolic while acknowledging its theological message, could one not do the same for Genesis 2? But, clearly, Dr. Lejeune has too high a respect for science to be considered with this first group. I will come back to his views later.

Positivism and Materialism: A Challenge to Religion

In the second form of conflict, it is religion that is challenged in the name of science. *Positivism* asserts that science is the only reliable form of understanding. Science starts from reproducible public data. Theories are formulated, and their implications are tested against observations. In addition to empirical fit, the criteria of coherence, comprehensiveness, and fruitfulness influence choice among theories. Religious beliefs are not acceptable, in this view, because religion lacks such data, testing, and criteria. Science alone is objective, reliable, universal, and progressive. I take positivism, then, to be a statement about methods of inquiry.

Materialism goes further and asserts that only the entities with which science deals are real. It makes metaphysical claims about reality and not just epistemological claims about methods. At the most fundamental level, science deals with matter (or perhaps matter and energy); the materialist believes that all phenomena will eventually be explained in terms of the actions of material components. Materialism usually assumes some form of methodological reductionism, the claim that theories about phenomena of any kind can be reduced to theories about their component material parts.

Dr. Wilson defended materialism, though with several qualifications. He admitted that "religious belief is part of human nature and seemingly vital to social existence," and that religion is "too important to abandon." But, he also said that "traditional religious belief and scientific knowledge . . . are incompatible and mutually exclusive." In his book *On Human Nature*, he states that the power of religion will be gone forever when it is explained as a product of evolution. Would not this logic lead us to conclude that the power of science will also be gone forever when science, likewise, is explained as a product of evolution? Do evolutionary origins really have anything to do with the legitimacy of either field? I take it Dr. Wilson's basic position is that traditional religion has, in the past, served important functions that would now be better served if everyone adopted a philosophy of scientific materialism.

Is Dr. Wilson a reductionist? In some passages in his writing, he disavows reductionism and asserts—as Dr. Sperry does—that distinctive phenomena emerge at higher organizational levels. He says that the social sciences are far richer in content than the biological sciences. On the other hand, he states that biology is the key to human nature, and he gives it the preeminent role in explanation. For example, in *Sociobiology* he says that the social sciences and humanities are branches of biology, "the last branches of biology waiting to be included in the modern synthesis."[1] He says that the mind will be more precisely explained as an epiphenomenon of the neural machinery of the brain. The assumption here seems to be that there is only one acceptable type of explanation, therefore, that explanation in terms of evolutionary origins or biochemical activity excludes any other types of explanation. Explaining a phenomenon becomes a matter of "explaining it away," treating it as an epiphenomenon. Such reductionism was less evident in Dr. Wilson's remarks at this conference than in his earlier writing, and

---

[1] Edward O. Wilson, *Sociobiology* (Cambridge: Harvard University Press, 1978), p. 4.

he indicated in the discussion that some reformulation of his views has occurred in the last few years.

Is Dr. Wilson, then, a genetic determinist? I don't think so, because he acknowledges the plasticity of social behavior and the variability of cultural adaptation. Nevertheless, he gives the genes such a dominant role that he has great difficulty in allowing any scope for human freedom. He says that we have inherited a variety of genetically programmed emotional reactions, and that we must chose from among them which responses we wish to favor and which we wish to curtail. How do we make such choices? Not by our values, I take it, for they are also under genetic control.

Can we, then, derive a set of ethical principles from biological knowledge alone? I have problems with the use of such ethical terms as *altruism* and *selfishness* to characterize animal or insect behavior. For example, Dr. Wilson describes the self-sacrifice of social insects as "altruistic" because it benefits other insects that are genetically related. But, surely, we call self-sacrifice by human beings "altruistic" only if it is intentional, not if the benefit to others is an unintended consequence of our actions. I will suggest later that science can indeed show us the constraints within which human action is possible, and it can show us the consequences of our actions. But, it cannot establish the basic principles of ethical choice. So, I think Dr. Wilson presented us with a strong challenge to traditional forms of religion and ethics, though I was impressed by the geniality and openness with which he did it.

SCIENCE AND RELIGION IN INDEPENDENCE

Differing Methods, Attitudes, and Functions

One way to avoid all conflicts between science and religion is to insist that they are distinct, separate, independent enterprises. Each has its legitimate methods that can be justified in its own distinctive ways. Science is based on human observation and reason, while religion is based on divine revelation of other types of truth essentially unrelated to science. It is said that science is based on reason, while religion is based on faith. The two fields also require contrasting attitudes. Science requires detachment and impersonal objectivity, while religion requires personal involvement. Among recent philosophers, the linguistic analysts have stressed the differing functions of various types of language. The functions of scientific language are prediction, control, and technical application. The functions of religious language include ritual, ethical encouragement, and personal reorientation. Religion is a way of life aimed at the transformation of the person.

In these interpretations, religion and science are autonomous realms of thought that should be kept in watertight compartments. Correctly understood, they cannot conflict, but neither can they support each other or benefit from dialogue. Each is selective and has its limitations. Every discipline abstracts from the totality of experience those features in which it is interested. Eddington told a delightful parable about a man studying deep-sea life, using a net with a three-inch mesh. After bringing up repeated samples, the man concludes that there are no deep-sea fish less than three inches in length. Eddington believed that science is selective and therefore cannot claim that its picture of reality is complete.

Differing Questions, Objects, and Experiences

Science and religion not only use differing methods, it is said, but differ in content because they have differing objects of study. Science asks "how questions," questions about causes and structures, whereas religion asks "why questions," questions about meanings and purposes. Philosophers have analyzed the concept of explanation and have argued that there are various types of explanation, depending on one's goals and reasons for inquiry. The object of inquiry in science is the world of nature. The objects of inquiry in religion are said to be God and the self. Science portrays facts; religion elucidates values. Again, the two realms of thought arise from contrasting types of experience. The basic experience in science is lawful regularity among observations. The basic experience in religion is personal transformation—the transition from guilt, anxiety, and brokenness to forgiveness, peace, and wholeness. Science and religion, then, can avoid conflict if each stays in its own domain.

I think that, in the end, Dr. Dyson adopts an option we will take up later, but some of his remarks seem to lend support to the "independence" thesis. He spoke of the intolerance of some biologists in the creationist controversy and the need for humility since "neither side has a monopoly on the truth." He said that science and metascience use "two complementary styles of explanation," and he proposed that science is limited and restricted in its scope. He held, for example, that questions of purpose and design are excluded from science but not from philosophy.

Fr. McMullin emphasized the idea of independence, though with some qualifications. The doctrine of creation, he said, is not an explanation of cosmological beginnings but an assertion of the world's absolute dependence on God in every moment. He states: "As a first approximation, let us say that the sciences deal with the world, and theology with God"—though he granted that this is an over-simplification. Here is another quotation: "Augustine effectively distinguished between two orders of cause or explanation; each is complete in itself, but each also complements the other in a distinctive way." Fr. McMullin held that the sequence of natural causes is complete, and that God's role is to sustain the whole sequence. He was critical of natural theology, physicotheology, and the argument from design because they seek God in the unexplained gaps in scientific explanations. He saw this as dangerous, both because the gaps tend to be closed by new scientific advances, and because, at best, such arguments would only lead to a cosmic force, not to the transcendent biblical God who is never located in nature. He criticized Teilhard de Chardin and Whitehead on similar grounds.

Fr. McMullin concluded that science is not totally irrelevant to theology, though the only examples of relevance he gave were from the social sciences. In the discussion period, he did express appreciation for Teilhard's sense of a unitary evolutionary process, and he thought that even Aquinas might have welcomed that. But on the whole, Fr. McMullin sees few connections between science and theology.

In response, I would suggest that one can interpret Teilhard in more than one way. He does, indeed, sometimes sound as if he is writing natural theology, trying to draw theological conclusions from nature alone, or giving a new argument from design. But, looking at his life and writings as a whole, I believe his project was rather to integrate ideas from two sources: his scientific and religious background and experience. I see it primarily as a theology of nature rather than as a natural theology. Certainly, neither Teilhard nor Whitehead are guilty of locating God in nature. They both emphasize God's immanence, but they do not neglect transcendence. Fr. McMullin, on the other hand, stresses "absolute transcendence" and has much less to say about immanence.

There is another question here to which I do not have an easy answer. The Bible talks about the God who acts. How do we understand this if we don't want to posit God's intervention in gaps in the causal sequences of nature? Do we speak of God's role only as sustaining those causal sequences, with perhaps an occasional miraculous suspension of natural laws? Fr. McMullin says that God is responsible equally and uniformly for all events. Is the particularity of divine action then replaced by divine concurrence with natural causes in the execution of a totally predetermined plan? Or, can we talk about a continuing creation in which new creatures are brought into being? Are temporality and human freedom unreal to God since every event is already part of the divine plan, or are there genuine options open until we decide?

Thomistic philosophers have, of course, wrestled with these questions for centuries, but I am not altogether satisfied with their answers. Some physicists have proposed that God controls history by determining events at the subatomic level. The laws of quantum physics predict only the probability of an event within a range of possible events, but God might determine the event exactly. An alternative proposed by the process philosophers is that God's action occurs not in gaps within the scientific account but in the "within of things," the interior life of every entity, with which science does not deal. That, too, has its difficulties (which I will mention shortly) but, on the whole, it seems to be a more promising approach.

In general, then, I find much that is valid in the "independence" position. It is indeed a good first approximation. It is a useful strategy for responding to both types of conflict mentioned earlier. I believe, however, that it overdraws the contrasts between science and religion and neglects some significant parallels. It also neglects some areas where science and religion can fruitfully interact. In their preoccupation with personal salvation, many theologians have given too little attention to the created order. If theology has little to say about nature, it will not be surprising if nature is treated as an object to be exploited. The meaning of personal life, which is indeed a central concern of religion, depends, in part, on belief in a meaningful cosmos.

SCIENCE AND RELIGION IN INTERACTION

Methodological Parallels

Despite their differences, both the positions outlined so far draw very strong contrasts between the methods of science and the methods of religion. But, such absolute contrasts have been questioned. There are alternative portrayals of both science and religion.

One of the changes on the scientific side is a new appraisal of the role of the observer. In the older view, an observer is detached and separate from what he or she is observing. In the new view, the observer is a participant, inseparable from the process of observation. The participant observer, who influences what is observed, is now acknowledged not only in ecology and in the social sciences but also in quantum physics. We cannot talk about the quantum world in itself but only about its interaction with us. Dr. Dyson mentioned that Einstein still believed in an objective world, independent of human thought and observation, but added that most physicists today no longer accept this view. I am not saying that we can equate the kind of participation that occurs in science with that that occurs in religion, but I am suggesting that the earlier contrast between objective detachment and personal involvement was overdrawn.

Another parallel I have explored in some of my writings is the role of *conceptual models* in both science and religion. I have suggested that the Bohr model of the atom, the complementary wave and particle models of the electron, or the more recent models of quarks are not to be taken as literal pictures of reality. Neither are they useful fictions or physiological aids that can be discarded once we have a mathematical theory, as the instrumentalists hold, for the model is a continuing source of modifications to the theory. I have defended critical realism, the view that conceptual models are partial and inadequate representation of what cannot be directly observed. They are used to interpret selected aspects of the behavior of a complex system for particular purposes. Similarly, religious models, such as personal and impersonal models of God, are used to interpret distinctive types of religious experience. Religious models are neither literal pictures nor useful fictions; they, too, are partial and inadequate ways of imagining what cannot be directly observed. There are many biblical metaphors of God as potter or as rock and a few feminine images of God. Some of the metaphors are more systematically developed as models, for example, God as Father and God as King. If there were time, we could explore similarities and differences in comparing the roles of models in science and in religion.

What about the question of testing and verification in science and in religion? Broad scientific paradigms are very difficult to verify or falsify. No book since World War II has had more influence in the philosophy of science than Thomas Kuhn's *The Structure of Scientific Revolutions*. Kuhn defined a paradigm as a cluster of conceptual, metaphysical, and methodological presuppositions embodied in a tradition of scientific work, such as Newtonian mechanics or quantum physics. Through standard examples, students learn what kinds of entity there are in the world and what procedures are suitable for studying them. Even the data are paradigm-dependent. With a new paradigm, the old data are reinterpreted and seen in new ways, and new kinds of data are sought. According to Kuhn, a paradigm shift is a "radical transformation of the scientific imagination," a "scientific revolution" that is not the product of experimental data alone.

There are no clear rules for applying the scientific criteria mentioned earlier or for judging their relative importance. Consider the criterion of empirical fit. Should one conclude that data that do not fit a theory falsify the theory? Or, should the discrepancy be resolved by introducing an *ad hoc* auxiliary hypothesis? Or, should the discordant data simply be set aside as an unexplained anomaly? Such a decision cannot be made by applying a rule; it is an act of judgment by a scientific community. A paradigm defines a community that works together within a set of shared assumptions. A paradigm, even more than a theory, is resistant to falsification, but an accumulation of anomalies and *ad hoc* hypotheses, together with a new and fruitful conceptual scheme, may eventually lead to a paradigm shift.

Religious traditions can also be looked on as communities that share a common paradigm. The paradigm is based on shared data, such as religious experience and a memory of key stories and events in Scripture, but the interpretation of the data is even more paradigm-dependent than in the case of science. There is a greater use of *ad hoc* assumptions to reconcile such apparent anomalies as the existence of evil, so religious paradigms are even more resistant to falsification. But, paradigm shifts in religion do occur, both in major revolutions such as the Protestant Reformation and in the life of individuals who adopt a new religious paradigm.

Some interpreters have gone even further in stressing the influence of cultural assumptions and social interests on both religious and scientific beliefs. Third World liberation theology insists that economic and social interests affect everyone's interpretation of Scripture. Feminist theologians hold that male perspectives have influenced the models of God that theologians have developed in the past. Similarly, some philosophers of science, especially those sympathetic to recent work in the sociology of knowledge, assert that the directions of scientific development and even its conceptual frameworks are influenced by cultural assumptions. For example, Third World scientists note that most of the world's research effort is directed to the diseases and problems prevalent in affluent societies. Feminist scientists note that Darwin and his early followers focused on struggle and competition, neglecting cooperative behavior as a factor in evolutionary survival. They suggest that this oversight is not unrelated to the fact that the biologists were men in a competitive culture. I think we must take seriously these critics who point to the social context of all our thought, though I think they go too far in stressing the cultural relativity of knowledge.

In describing certain similarities between science and religion, one need not ignore the differences, though sometimes the latter turn out to be differences in degree rather than absolute contrasts. I would still defend the distinctiveness of religious methods, questions, and experiences. I would not claim that religious beliefs are amenable to strict empirical testing, but I would hope for some of the same spirit of inquiry found in science. The scientific criteria of coherence, comprehensiveness, and fruitfulness have their parallels in religious thought. Theology is a human enterprise that can develop and grow and be open to new insights, including insights derived from science. As Cardinal Newman pointed out, there can be significant doctrinal development over time.

Religious Views Derived from Science

Historically, there has been a variety of attempts to derive religious beliefs from scientific evidence. In the Catholic Church, natural theology has, of course, been a strong tradition, separate from Christian theology based on revelation. While the classical argument from design appealed to well-known features of the world, by Newton's time, it made extensive use of scientific findings. After Darwin, it was sometimes reformulated so that it referred not to the separate design of each species but to the design of the whole evolutionary process through which species came into being. Dr. Dyson gave a cautious endorsement of this kind of design argument as an extension of the anthropic principle, the idea that the physical constants that determine the very early history of the cosmos seem to be extraordinarily fine-tuned to produce conditions in which intelligent life could emerge.

This form of the argument from design is not subject to Fr. McMullin's warning against making theological use of explanatory gaps that may be closed by future scientific advances. To be sure, the physical constants upon which the anthropic principle depends may turn out not to be arbitrary but, rather, to be determined by a more fundamental theory—perhaps the Grand Unification Theory currently being sought or a future theory of super symmetry that will integrate gravity with electromagnetic and nuclear forces. But, that will only push the question back a stage: How can we account for the unified theory that made life possible?

In the central part of his paper, Dr. Lejeune seemed to be giving us the older form of the argument from design. He made much of the gaps in the neo-Darwinian account, the unexplained phenomena, the rapidity of evolutionary change, the difficulty in accounting for speciation. He said that with random mutations "the time required would be immeasurably greater than geological time." He questioned whether blind chance could produce the eye. The parable of the Detroit auto factory implied an intelligent designer as the source of novelty, in evolution as in Detroit. But, in the question period, he said that he looked to better scientific theories, rather than God's activity, to fill those unexplained gaps. He said that such theories would have not theological implications.

There would be no difficulty, I suggest, in adding new features to the neo-Darwinian account. For instance, there is evidence that gene transposition is more frequent than had been supposed, and this may well be another source of novelty. One could add Dr. Lejeune's proposal about the three-dimensional interaction of chromosomes though, as Dr. Wilson said, there isn't much evidence for it. But, other ideas that Dr. Lejeune presented are more problematic. He said that protohorses, the ancestors of the horse, were trying to become more horse-like. If chromosomes change in anticipation of future adaptive need, this would indicate a future-oriented purposiveness, an orthogenesis at the molecular level, which is hard to reconcile with current theories or with the fact that the vast majority of mutations are harmful. Are there philosophical, if not theological, reasons for advancing such a proposal? I am not clear about either Dr. Lejeune's proposal or its implications.

Let us turn to Dr. Sperry's thought as a religious view that claims to be derived from science. We saw earlier that a mechanistic and reductionistic view of science has led some people to reject all religious beliefs. But, Dr. Sperry's holistic, mentalistic, and emergent understanding leads him to a form of pantheism. In a recent article, he advocates what he calls "pantheism made palatable."[2] It is more appropriate, he suggests, to equate God with the laws and forces of the universe if these laws and forces are not mechanical, blind, and controlled by necessity and chance but are, instead, seen to be vital, creative, and directional. Dr. Sperry's view of human nature, allowing an important place for consciousness and free will among higher-level emergent phenomena, is closer than Dr. Wilson's view to the traditional religious understanding.

I would like to see a more thorough philosophical analysis of the differences between a reductionist and an emergentist interpretation of the scientific data. The change from a mechanistic to a holistic perspective is just the kind of paradigm shift that cannot be readily decided on empirical grounds alone because it involves looking at the same data in a new way. But, I think the holistic paradigm is beginning to vindicate itself both as a fruitful basis for scientific research and as a framework for integrating the scientific understanding of human behavior with our firsthand experience as human beings. The idea of causal influences operating from the top down among hierarchical levels of organization is particularly promising, and it gains some support from systems theory. However, I am puzzled by Dr. Sperry's hostility to quantum theory. He evidently thinks it would be reductionistic to give too much attention to quantum theory, which he looks on as part of the older mechanistic paradigm. But, many people who share his philosophy of emergence welcome quantum theory as part of the new paradigm precisely because it departs from microdeterminism. The presence of indeterminacy at the bottom seems to diminish the control from the bottom up and to allow more opportunity for top-down control.

Integration of Ideas from Science and Religion

Instead of trying to derive religious beliefs from science, I would advocate an integration of ideas coming from science and from religion considered as relatively independent sources. The ideas from the two sources interact because they are related to each other

---

[2]Roger Sperry, "Changed Concepts of Brain and Consciousness," *Perkins Journal* (Summer 1983): 24.

at crucial points. Our understanding of how God and the self are related to nature will inevitably be affected by our understanding of nature. Science is, therefore, relevant to specific doctrines such as the doctrine of creation and doctrines about human nature. Science is also relevant to the elaboration of an inclusive and coherent metaphysical system. I take metaphysics to be the search for the most general set of categories applicable to all types of event and experience, including events and experiences important in both science and religion. Both can contribute to a coherent vision of reality. One of the nice things about speaking to a Catholic group is that I don't have to defend metaphysics as such. I can directly raise the question of whether Thomistic metaphysics, which was so heavily indebted to Aristotle, offers the most suitable set of categories for today.

First, let me ask: What contribution can religion make to science? Historians have wondered why modern science arose in the Judaeo-Christian West among all world cultures. A good case can be made that the doctrine of creation helped to set the stage for the scientific enterprise. Both Greek and biblical thought asserted that the world is orderly and intelligible. But, only biblical thought held that the world's order is contingent. It didn't have to be as it is, so you have to observe it rather than trying to deduce its structure from necessary principles. Moreover, while nature is real and good, it is not itself divine, as many ancient cultures held. You are, therefore, free to experiment on nature. The founders of modern science felt that in their inquiries they were thinking God's thoughts after him. Historically, this seems to be true, but there are two cautions for today. One is that the same desacralization of nature that encouraged scientific study also contributed to subsequent exploitation of nature—along with many other economic and cultural forces, to be sure. Second, once science proved its power, it could be justified by its own success. Russian scientists and many American scientists obviously do first-rate work without theistic assumptions. So, today I see the main contribution of religion to science in the area of ethical sensitivity.

The contribution in the reverse direction, from science to religion, occurs mainly in discussing the relation of God and humanity to nature. Dr. Dyson asked how God's freedom or human freedom might be correlated with chance and uncertainty at the quantum level. I'm not quite sure where he came out concerning God's freedom. At one point, he described the unpredictability of matter and concluded: "We have learned that matter is weird stuff. It is weird enough so that it does not limit God's freedom to make it do what he pleases." This might mean that God controls what happens within those quantum uncertainties. The outcome appears as chance to us, but it is really determined by God in accordance with the divine plan. This would be a new way of expressing a more traditional understanding of predestination. But, he later agreed with Hartshorne that chance is real to God. Dr. Dyson said: "God is not omniscient. He grows with the universe and learns as it develops. Chance is a part of his plan. He uses it as we do to achieve his ends." I take it this is the direction in which Dr. Dyson's thought moves. It is an example of theological reflection that takes seriously an important aspect of current science, for chance is a concept found not just in quantum physics but in evolutionary biology and elsewhere. The biochemist and Anglican theologian Arthur Peacocke, among others, has written extensively about the representation of God's action in a world of law and chance.[3]

Dr. Dyson makes the interesting proposal that we think of God's relation to the world as analogous to the relation of mind to body in human beings. In other words, the world is God's body and God is the world's mind. Some linguistic philosophers have made similar proposals. We can describe a human action, such as moving my arm, in terms of muscle contractions and physiological processes, or we can describe it in terms of intentions and purposes: I may have been exercising or waving to someone. Similarly, we can describe cosmic history in the language of physical causes or in the language of divine intentions. I wonder, however, if the world has the kind of unity an integrated organism possesses, as the analogy would require. I see greater promise in the process philosophers and theologians—Whitehead, Hartshorne, or Teilhard—who insist that God is intimately involved in the world but must be distinguished from it. Fr. Bracken referred to some of Whitehead's ideas in his response to Dr. Sperry, and Fr. King, who responded to Dr. Wilson, is sympathetic to Teilhard's thought. Let me touch very briefly on how some of the themes of this conference might be taken to support a process view.

What are the changing views of nature that might affect our understanding of God's relation to nature? At the risk of oversim-

---

[3]Arthur Peacocke, *Creation and the World of Science* (Oxford: Oxford University Press, 1978), ch. 3.

plification, I point to four characteristics of the medieval view of
nature.[4] (1) It was a *static order;* there was change within it and
directionality in human history, but the basic forms were all fixed.
(2) It was *teleological* in that every creature expressed both the divine
purpose and its own built-in goals. (3) It was *substantive;* that is,
the components were separate mental and material substances. (4)
It was *hierarchical,* with each lower form serving the higher (God/
man/woman/animal/plant). It was a single unified order, with all
the parts harmoniously working together for a common purpose
(see Table below).

VIEWS OF NATURE

Medieval	*Newtonian*	*Twentieth-Century*
Static order	Change as rearrangement	Evolutionary, dynamic, emergent
Teleological	Deterministic	Chance and law
Substantive	Atomistic	Relational, ecological, interdependent
Hierarchical	Reductionistic	Systems and wholes

MODELS OF GOD'S RELATION TO NATURE

Monarchial (ruler/subject)	Deistic (clockmaker/clock)	Process (cosmic society)

The Newtonian world was different at each of these points. (1)
It incorporated change, but only *change as rearrangement* of unchanging components. (2) It was *deterministic* rather than teleological.
Mechanical causes, not purposes, determined all events. (3) It was
atomistic in taking separate particles rather than substances to be
the basic reality of nature. (4) It was *reductionistic* rather than hi-

---

[4]See, for example, N. Max Wildiers, *The Theologian and His Universe* (New York:
Seabury Press, 1982).

erarchical since the mechanisms at the lowest level determined events.

Twentieth-century science, as we have seen in these talks, departs significantly from the Newtonian conception of nature. (1) Nature is now understood to be *evolutionary, dynamic, and emergent.* It is historical throughout, and its basic forms have changed radically. Successive levels of organization have appeared (matter, life, mind, culture). (2) In place of determinism, we have a complex combination of *chance and law* (including statistical laws). (3) Nature is understood to be *relational, ecological, and interdependent.* Reality is constituted by relationships rather than by separate substances or separate particles externally related. (4) Reduction continues to be fruitful in the analysis of the separate components of systems, but attention is also given to *systems and wholes* themselves. Distinctive concepts are used to explain the higher-level activities of systems, from organisms to ecosystems. There is a hierarchy of levels, rather than a hierarchy of beings.

What models of *God's relation to nature* fit with each of these views of nature? The dominant medieval model was *monarchial,* though other models were used, especially for God's relation to humanity. God's relation to a teleological and hierarchical world was taken to be analogous to a ruler's relation to subjects. The dominant model in Newton's day was *deistic.* If nature was a clock, then God was the clockmaker. There is a variety of models today, but I want to look especially at the *process* model. Here, nature is seen as an interacting network of beings; God is not part of that network but is the preeminent member of a cosmic society that includes God and the world—not a democratic society, therefore, yet one that is neither as hierarchical as the medieval system nor as mechanical as the Newtonian.'

The medieval model emphasized God's absolute power and freedom. Critics of this model have found it difficult to reconcile with human freedom and responsibility and with the existence of evil and chance in the world. The deistic model affirms God's power in constructing the world machine, but, thereafter, God has no role because the machine runs itself. The process theologians portray a God who is neither omnipotent nor powerless, a God of persuasion rather than coercion or inactivity. The process God does not predetermine or control the world but participates in it at all levels to orchestrate the spontaneity of all beings to achieve a richer coherence. God does not act directly, and nothing that happens is God's act alone; instead, God acts along with other causes and influences the creatures to act. God does not intervene sporadically from outside but, rather, is present in the unfolding of every event.

A Christian view of God's relation to nature must, of course, be faithful to the biblical understanding as well as to changing views of nature. As noted earlier, there are many models of God in the Bible. God as King is one of them, and many of the features of the monarchial model are surely appropriate. God as potter is a biblical image, though not a systematic model, and perhaps some features of the deistic model can be retained, despite its limitations. Without the model of God as Father, it would leave us with only an intelligent designer, too distant for personal relationship. The process model of a God of persuasion rather than coercion is particularly consonant with our understanding of the cross and the power of love. Models of God's relation to nature must be consistent with models of God's relation to humanity, and we would have to go on to ask about our understanding of grace and redemption. Creation and redemption are two aspects of a single divine activity.

We should not expect science and its view of nature to contribute too much to theology, for other sources—Scripture and religious experience—are more important in any attempt to speak of God. But, I would suggest that, just as Aquinas brought Scripture into relationship with the best philosophical and scientific thought of his day, we must do the same in our day, building on the past but not being restricted to it.

One final comment. If we had time, we could trace views of the relation of ethics to science through the same threefold outline that I presented earlier. Some people find conflicts between science and ethics, others see them as totally unrelated, and still others hold that they interact—and again there are several kinds of interaction. The Catholic tradition has always found a place for natural law as well as natural theology. I would argue that science can show us the biological and psychological constraints within which human action is possible. It can help us to understand our interdependence with other creatures on this amazing planet. It can show us that our actions have consequences distant in space and time, so we must broaden the scope of our ethical concern. Science is therefore relevant to ethics, but I would not look to science for the establishment of fundamental ethical norms such as social justice, individual freedom, or even respect for nature, for these are rooted in our understanding of the character of ultimate reality. In ethics, as in theology, I think the most fruitful dialogue between scientists and theologians can occur if interaction is encouraged but the distinctive contribution of each enterprise is respected.

Discussion

CARDINAL LAW: I regret that I must leave the chair to take part in a press conference scheduled for this hour. But, I leave it in most competent hands. Bishop Melczek has agreed to stand in for me.

BISHOP MELCZEK: Are there any group reactions to Dr. Barbour's fine summation?

FR. MORACZEWSKI: Our topic of discussion turned into a question. Is truth verified in the Church by authority and in science by consensual validation of evidence? Or, does one find both authority and consensual validation in both religion and science?

We suggest three ways in which religion contributes to the scientific enterprise. First, religion suggests to science issues upon which research is particularly important. Second, religion introduces ethical considerations that partly govern how scientific truth will be applied to human affairs. I think Pope John Paul II, in one of his early talks to the Pontifical Academy of Sciences, distinguished between pure science, where truth itself is the ultimate judge, and applied science, where ethical considerations have to operate in the interaction with human welfare. Third, religion can contribute a lively appreciation of historical perspective in science. Sometimes modern young scientists act as though science began with their research. It was Newton who said, "If I have seen further, it is because I have stood on the shoulders of giants." We need to remember on whose shoulders we are standing.

As to science's contribution to religion and the pursuit of truth, we would underscore the importance of the scientific mindset that asks, "What is the evidence?" A Swedish physiologist I knew was always asking this very question. Once, I was alone in an elevator with him. There was a story in the newpaper he was reading about a person going to Lourdes for a cure. He looked at me in my collar and said, "Reverend, is there going to be a cure or not? Predict!" If I hadn't been so startled, I could have answered, "What kind of evidence will you accept?" Science suggests to religion the importance of maintaining an objective stance, a kind of honesty. Having worked in both the scientific and theological fields, I feel that theologians are sometimes influenced by factors not directly pertinent to the search for truth. Science reminds us to focus on the objective and honest approach to truth.

Our group favors the third alternative Dr. Barbour presented: fruitful interaction between religion and science. We look forward to more interaction, to the benefit of both disciplines and, ultimately, all humanity.

DR. PATRICK BYRNE: In our search for a controversial subject, we happened upon human sexuality. First, a couple of remarks about context. In a culture whose thinking and discourse is frequently irrational, the Catholic Church's position on contraception comes to sound irrational, too. In other words, in an irrational society, reason can sound irrational. Further, the culture misunderstands celibacy. One of the celibate members of our group reported that once, at a meeting, a non-Catholic scientist asked him: "Isn't the Church's promotion of institutional celibacy antihuman?"

Under the circumstances, it seems clear that sexuality is an important topic for science and religion to explore. We must work toward some resolution of major issues. There is much in Catholic tradition that can respond to the questions that are likely to arise, that can respond to the cultural climate in which we are living.

There are two different functions of reason that are relevant in the area of human sexuality. One is scientific reason, as such, and the other is *prudentia*, practical moral judgment. This distinction is helpful because in modern discourse there is no ready means of eliciting what light *prudentia* might shed on the discussion of Catholic teaching.

The first task in establishing dialogue between people of science and people of religion is to distinguish what scientists know as scientists—what they know insofar as they are following well-grounded and widely accepted principles of scientific methodology and verification—from the broad range of things that scientists know as human beings and for which there is no scientific verification. To illustrate, a good deal of what the speakers have given us has not been scientific knowledge, but what Fr. King called a philosophy or world view.

This distinction is particularly important in a culture where aberrant, and indeed pathological, thought is rampant as regards human sexuality. The culture assumes, for example, that there can be no reasonable sacrifice of one's sexual desires, which often makes sexuality a very sad or dangerous thing. We should accept scientists' pronouncements when based on scientific research but not when these pronouncements are based in the cultural climate.

The second task is to learn what scientists as scientists actually know about sexuality. Aristotle turned from the variety of opinions current in his own Athenian culture to the pivotal question of human function when trying to give a normative grounding for a science of ethics. We should first ask: "What do biologists know as biologists about the facts and functions of sexuality?" Then: "What do scientists as scientists know about the distinctively human aspects of sexuality?"

With this latter question, we leave the realm of the natural sciences and enter that of the human sciences. Here, a particular difficulty arises. In a certain sense, all data are equally valid in the natural sciences, but in the human sciences the data are human behaviors, and not all human behaviors follow human nature. Some are aberrations of human nature. Thus, the problem immediately arises of sorting out data on human nature and data on human aberration. Psychology, anthropology, and sociology can make significant contributions to this study.

Revealed religion can enter the discussion at this point, broadening our understanding of sexuality to include not only the biological and human but the supernatural as well. Religion can explore the ways in which sexuality shares in God's plan.

The third and last *desideratum* I will mention is to come to some contemporary understanding of finality. It has been taken for granted that final causation is "out." Final causation understood as some unverifiable and unobservable *telos* that sits inside a photon, cell, or chromosome and pushes it in a predetermined direction is indeed not compatible with modern scientific thought. But, this is not the only meaning of final causation, particularly as it concerns sexual morality.

MSGR. JOHN NIENSTEDT: Our starting point was the fine *schema* Dr. Barbour provided on the abuse of nature and our understanding of how God relates to nature. We asked ourselves whether our present concept of natural law is adequate in light of the modern dynamic view of nature. Nature, after all, should be the basis of natural law.

We didn't want to be too abstract, so we concretized our discussion around the morality of *in vitro* fertilization and embryo transfer. In this context, how would the scientific and theological communities understand separating the marital embrace and the act of conception or, if you will, the lovemaking and baby-making aspects of the marriage act, as "natural"? Does the scientific community see *in vitro* fertilization as a sort of organ bypass in which the fallopian tube is rendered irrelevant, much as a coronary bypass replaces an artery? Or, does this procedure lead to a brave new world, where the most intimate form of human communication is disturbed? Our questions for the theological community would be: "How does *in vitro* fertilization affect the marriage bond?" "From a theological perspective, how should one characterize the achievement of fertility by this means?" "How can we say that it is predicated on human nature?" Our group didn't resolve anything, but it became clear to us that our understanding of natural law may need to be refined.

DR. BELA PIACSEK: I am an endocrinologist, a reproductive biologist. I have spent the last twenty years doing research in such areas as puberty and the causes of puberty. I keep hearing the word *sexuality* but, to this point, no one has given a real definition of that word. We can talk about biological sexuality and human sexuality but, unless we define our terms, I don't think we can decide what science's contribution, religion's contribution, or behavioral science's contribution is. *Sexuality* can refer simply to what makes us male and female. Beyond sex determination, we can talk about the physiological and anatomical bases of sexual function. We can get one step higher and talk about sexual behaviors, some of which are definitely physiologically controlled, hormonally induced and determined. We can go further and talk about moral codes regarding sexual behavior, where I think the contribution of science will become very limited. There is a need for definition if we are to agree on what scientific and religious insights are relevant to this topic.

BISHOP MELCZEK: You have highlighted a problem that has come up over and over again, that is, the definition of terms. Clearly, the scientific community and religious communities do not use the same terms in the same way.

SR. LAURA L. LANDEN, OP: I would like to return to Dr. Barbour's talk and make some comments on it both as a teacher of philosophy and natural science and as a student of the history of science. I respect his knowledge of science and his writings in the methodology and history of science. But, I would like to raise an objection to Dr. Barbour's characterization of the medieval world view as static; the Newtonian world view as recognizing change in the sense of rearrangement; and the modern world view as process-oriented, dynamic, and evolutionary. I think each of these three historical periods, and the period of classical Greek science as well, exhibit more subtleties than Dr. Barbour admits. I'm sure theologians would say that the models of God are also much more nuanced in these historical periods than was suggested.

With regard to the methodology of science and the Kuhnian analysis of paradigm shift as explanatory of the way in which scientific enterprise develops, I have read carefully and use *The Structure of Scientific Revolutions* in teaching the philosophy of science, but I have serious problems with it. While Kuhn raises some good questions, he has difficulty accounting for science as a search for truth and as an understanding of this truth grounded in the study of our common world. I am not sure that Kuhn's paradigm shifts adequately capture the essence of science.

PARTICIPANT: I agree with Dr. Barbour's statement that religion can influence science by giving scientists a greater moral sensitivity to the consequences of the work they are doing. But, religion may exercise another sort of influence as well. Science's enormous growth in the last eighty years, I think, has placed it on the heights. It has yet to find its proper place in the fabric of human culture. I think religion will be one of the strongest forces in helping it to find that place.

FR. BENEDICT ASHLEY: It is very important to think about how the tension between science and the Christian religion arose. It is a peculiar development because the originators of modern science were mostly Catholic Christians and orthodox Protestant Christians. By and large, they thought science would be a great help to religion; this belief motivated a lot of their work. In their writings, some say that science is important because it will teach us more about God.

How, then, did science become a kind of rival to religion? I think the explanation lies in the religious wars that scarred Europe, when modern science was gaining strength, in the latter half of the seventeenth century. Those religious wars between Catholics and Protestants disillusioned many of the intelligentsia with Christianity. They began seeking an alternative, which they, at first, thought could be found in a universal natural religion—deism. The founders of the United States largely shared this point of view.

Over the years, interest in natural religion waned and the disillusioned intelligentsia, still trying to find a satisfactory world view and value system, chose to develop one of their own. The new religion they invented was humanism. After two hundred years, it dominates the Western world, or at least the Western elites, and is responsible for the pervasive secularization of our culture.

There is a lot to be said for humanism; it has done a great deal to secure basic rights for people at large. Its fundamental assumption, however, is that God is unknowable. While we may have personal opinions about God, there is no way to verify them, no way to bring them into the realm of objective, public knowledge. Science must supply our knowledge, and technology must take the place of prayer, the sacraments, and dependence on God. Thus, we will solve our problems.

Under pressure of this line of thought, the scientific community has gradually taken on its present agnostic aspect. Science in general—whatever individual scientists may believe—treats religion as a purely private matter, something not subject to objective discussion. Thus, the humanists have co-opted science and use it as a weapon against Christianity. And, we have made the terrible mistake of letting them do it. The establishment of regular dialogue between religion and science raises the great hope that Christians will realize that science belongs as much to us as to anybody else. We have as much right to offer philosophical and theological comment on scientific endeavor as do people of the humanist persuasion. As a matter of fact, beyond a dialogue with science, we need a dialogue with humanism. Humanism is a religion. If we can dialogue with the Buddhists and Muslims, why can't we dialogue with humanists in charity and in fairness?

It is important to recognize the reality we face. When we talk about religion and science, there is another world view involved besides the Christian one. Christianity and humanism each strives to interpret science, which is neutral as regards both, in a way congruent with its particular outlook. At this time in the West, humanism has the upper hand.

BISHOP MELCZEK: A number of important issues are being raised. Let's give Dr. Barbour a chance to comment.

DR. BARBOUR: Sr. Laura Landen raised some important questions about my *schema*. I am never quite sure how much detail and how much editorializing is appropriate when my assignment is to

summarize. Certainly, the *schema* is an oversimplification. I agree
that the extent to which the medieval world view is static is open
to debate. There are many dynamic elements in it. Certainly, the
whole story of salvation gives history a directionality in Western
thought that is absent in Asian or Greek thought. All I meant was
that the medieval world is one where the basic entities do not
change.

I recently gave a seminar attended by a Dominican and a Fran-
ciscan, one representing a Thomistic view and one a process view.
The Thomist was driven to see all kinds of process themes in St.
Thomas, while the process theologian was able to accept much of
St. Thomas' perspective. So, I am not sure that one has to make
a hard and fast choice between these two views of reality. Nevertheless, particularly as regards nature, there is in the evolutionary
perspective an important sense of historical change that was absent
in the medieval world. History itself involves change, of course,
so there was dynamism in the medieval world, but nature was seen
either as emblematic of the supernatural realm or as a set of fixed
forms.

This recognition of the historicity of nature strikes me as an
important shift, partly because history brings to nature a temporal
dimension. It gives us another reason—in addition to the question
of human freedom—to see temporality as an important feature of
modern thought with which theology has to come to terms. The
fact that this sense of dynamic process receives little attention in
the medieval world view does not reflect any shortcoming in biblical
thought, which is historically oriented. Rather, it reflects the dom-
inance of Greek categories, particularly Platonic categories, in which
the eternal was the true and in which change was ignored in the
contemplation of eternal forms. I raise questions about the medieval
synthesis partly because some of the elements it drew from the
Greeks are in tension with elements it drew from biblical thought.
Greek thought was overly dominant at some points in the medieval
synthesis. In many ways, I find process philosophy more true to
the biblical understanding of a God who interacts with his creation.

Sr. Landen also mentioned paradigm shifts. Certainly, Kuhn's
ideas are often misused. Yet, they are bearing fruit in some interesting work. Several years ago, a conference was held at Tubingen
where Catholic and Protestant theologians discussed paradigm shifts
in Christianity. The participants found the paradigm framework a
useful way of looking at the kinds of changes that occur. Kuhn's

formulation has influenced scientists as well, emphasizing a number of features in science that had been neglected. Certainly, there are a number of schools of philosophy of science and some seem to fit the history of science, or different episodes in the history of science, better than others. When all is said and done, though, I find Kuhn's a useful framework.

Let me close by saying that the last three days have been fascinating. I very much appreciate the historical perspective that Fr. Ashley and Fr. McMullin have brought to us. The problems we have been dealing with are not new, although they take on a new force in an age where science is so dominant. We need to take science seriously, but we need not give it the last word. The scientists are in no position to tell theologians what the answers are.

BISHOP MELCZEK: I'm sorry to announce that our time is up. Archbishop Hickey, do you have any thoughts for us as we conclude this conference?

ARCHBISHOP HICKEY: I certainly hope you agree with me that these have been challenging and stimulating days of discussion and reflection. I hope, too, that our work together will prove to be a first step in developing and strengthening the relationship between religion and science. We have tried very honestly, all of us, to listen to one another and to respond. Your enthusiasm has encouraged me, as chairman of the Bishops' Committee on Human Values, to proceed with the planning of an ongoing dialogue. We see such dialogue as more than just an interesting interdisciplinary exercise. It is a real necessity.

I want to thank all of you for your participation. I pray that the Lord will continue to bless our mutual efforts. I pray that our labors will be of value for the Church and the whole human family. May the Lord's wisdom and love, so brilliantly reflected in nature, be ours in ever more abundant measure.

Appendix I

COMMITTEE ON HUMAN VALUES
NATIONAL CONFERENCE OF CATHOLIC BISHOPS
STATEMENT OF PURPOSE

> The conflicts which, at times, arose from undue influences of religious authorities on the development of scientific knowledge do not derive from the nature of reason and belief and, moreover, they now belong to the past. Should they again arise, a dialogue should be set up which is unprejudiced by undue passions. . . . Such a dialogue should, above all, try to clarify the problems in question and to discover a possible convergence of the various truths involved.

> When knowledge leads to the highest realities and, starting from them, tries to investigate all other domains of being, knowledge becomes wisdom (Pope John Paul II, *Address to the World of Culture at Fribourg University*, June 13, 1984).

The primary goal of the Committee on Human Values of the National Conference of Catholic Bishops is to establish ongoing discussion between the bishops and the American scientific community. By probing the ramifications of the relationship between religion and science, these discussions will help clear the air so that neither the religious nor the scientific communities is uncomfortable in the presence of the other.

The communication thus established is of the highest value. Both religion and science have insights to share on the great philosophical and practical questions of our time. Catholic theology must confront the spirit of scientific humanism in contemporary American culture, and Catholic moral values must be brought to bear on issues in science and technology. Wisdom lies where the truths of religion and science conjoin.

The Committee achieves its purpose by establishing and maintaining ongoing dialogue groups concerned with issues of theological and philosophical interest. It also refers scientific/technological advances to outside groups for study of their theological implications. Where appropriate, it uses the results of such consultation to comment on selected questions in association with other NCCB/USCC committees.

September 1986

Appendix II

LIST OF CONFERENCE PARTICIPANTS

Rev. Benedict Ashley, OP
Emeritus Professor
Aquinas Institute (St. Louis)

Most Rev. Robert J. Banks
Auxiliary Bishop of Boston

Dr. Ian G. Barbour
Professor of Religion
Carleton College

Dr. Elizabeth Letitia Beard
Professor of Biological Sciences
Loyola University
(New Orleans)

Dr. James A. Blachowicz
Associate Professor of Philosophy
Loyola University (Chicago)

Dr. Richard J. Blackwell
Professor of Philosophy
St. Louis University

Dr. Avrom Blumberg
Professor of Chemistry
DePaul University

Dr. Richard A. Boulet
Professor of Religious Studies
University of Dayton

Rev. Jospeh A. Bracken, SJ
Professor of Theology
Xavier University (Cincinnati)

Rev. Robert Brungs, SJ
Director
Institute for Theological Encounter with
Science and Technology
(St. Louis)

Dr. Patrick Byrne
Associate Professor of Philosophy
Boston College

Rev. Enrico Cantore, SJ
Director
World Institute for Scientific Humanism
Fordham University at Lincoln Center

Dr. Mary Lou Caspers
Associate Professor of Chemistry
University of Detroit

Most Rev. Walter A. Coggin, OSB
Former Abbot-Nullius
Belmont Abbey

Dr. Elizabeth Cole
Associate Professor of Psychology
Gonzaga University

Most Rev. Patrick R. Cooney
Auxiliary Bishop of Detroit

Dr. James B. Courtright
Professor of Biology
Marquette University

Dr. Benedict T. DeCicco
Professor and Director
Microbial Lab
The Catholic University of America

Dr. Dennis Doherty
Associate Professor of Theology
Marquette University

Sr. Rosemary Donley, SC, Ph.D.
Executive Vice-President
The Catholic University of America

Most Rev. Thomas A. Donnellan
Archbishop of Atlanta

Dr. Freeman Dyson
Professor of Physics
Institute for Advanced Study
Princeton University

Rev. Joseph Earley, SJ
Chairman
Department of Chemistry
Georgetown University

Most Rev. Edward M. Egan
Auxiliary Bishop of New York

Dr. William W. Eidson
Dean
College of Arts and Sciences
Loyola University
(New Orleans)

Dr. Lawrence Fagg
Professor of Physics
The Catholic University of America

John Collins Harvey, M.D.
Professor of Medicine
Georgetown University Hospital

Dr. Alice B. Hayes
Associate Academic
Vice-President
and Professor of Biology
Loyola University (Chicago)

Most Rev. James A. Hickey
Archbishop of Washington

Most Rev. James R. Hoffman
Bishop of Toledo

Most Rev. Howard J. Hubbard
Bishop of Albany

Dr. Paul Kenney
Professor of Physics
University of Notre Dame

Rev. Thomas King, SJ
Associate Professor of Theology
Georgetown University

Sr. Laura L. Landen, OP
Assistant Professor of Philosophy
Providence College

Bernard Cardinal Law
Archbishop of Boston

Dr. Frederick G. Lawrence
Associate Professor of Theology
Boston College

Dr. John Leahy
Associate Professor of Religious Studies
DePaul University

Dr. Jerome J. Lejeune
Executive Director
Institute de Progenese (Paris)

Rev. William E. Lori, S.T.D.
Secretary to the Archbishop
Archdiocese of Washington

Most Rev. George E. Lynch
Former Auxiliary Bishop of Raleigh

Most Rev. William E. McManus
Former Bishop of Fort Wayne-South Bend

Rev. Ernan McMullin
Director
Program in History and Philosophy of Science
University of Notre Dame

Most Rev. Dale J. Melczek
Auxiliary Bishop of Detroit

Dr. Virginia Merriam
Chairperson/Professor of Biology
Loyola Marymount University

Rev. Albert S. Moraczewski, OP
Regional Director
Pope John XXIII Center for
Medical-Moral Research (Houston)

Rev. Msgr. John C. Nienstedt
St. Regis Church
Birmingham, Michigan

Dr. James F. O'Brien
Professor of Philosophy
Villanova University

Dr. Alain Phares
Professor of Physics
Villanova University

Dr. Bela E. Piacsek
Professor of Biology
Marquette University

Dr. Robert Prusch
Professor and Chairman of Biology
Gonzaga University

Rev. Paul M. Quay, SJ
Research Professor in Philosophy
Loyola University (Chicago)

Most Rev. A. James Quinn
Auxiliary Bishop of Cleveland

Dr. Joan E. Roberts
Associate Professor of Chemistry
Fordham University at Lincoln Center

Dr. Robert John Russell
Director and Founder
Center for Theology and the Natural Sciences
Berkeley, California

Rev. James Salmon, SJ
Professor of Chemistry
Wheeling College

Dr. Edwin Schillinger
Professor of Physics
DePaul University

Dr. Patricia Schulz
Associate Professor of Biology
University of San Francisco

Dr. Irene T. Schulze
Professor of Microbiology
St. Louis University

Dr. Edward M. Sion
Associate Professor of Astronomy
Villanova University

Rev. James W. Skehan, SJ
Director
Weston Observatory
Boston College

Rev. Charles Skok, SJ
Chairman/Associate Professor
of Religious Studies
Gonzaga University

Bro. Anthony Smulders, CFMM, Ph.D.
Associate Dean of Science
Loyola Marymount University

Norma Sperry (Mrs. Roger W.)
and
Dr. Roger W. Sperry
Hixon Professor of Psychobiology
California Institute of Technology

Most Rev. Edmund C. Szoka
Archbishop of Detroit

Dr. Lawrence P. Ulrich
Professor and Chair of Philosophy
University of Dayton

Most Rev. Austin B. Vaughan
Auxiliary Bishop of New York

Dr. John F. Walsh
Professor of Psychology
Fordham University

Dr. James J. Walter
Associate Professor of Theology
Loyola University (Chicago)

Dr. Edward O. Wilson
Frank B. Baird, Jr., Professor of Science
Harvard University

Appendix III

ABOUT THE SPEAKERS

BENEDICT M. ASHLEY, OP, is Professor Emeritus of Moral Theology at the Aquinas Institute of Theology (St. Louis), where he was president from 1962-1969. He holds degrees from the University of Chicago; a Ph.D. in political science from the University of Notre Dame; a Ph.D. in philosophy from the Aquinas Institute of Theology; and a Master of Social Theology degree from the Dominican Order in Rome. Fr. Ashley is a Senior Fellow of the Pope John Center (Braintree, Massachusetts) and participates in the National Conference of Catholic Bishops dialogues with Methodists, as well as those with Scientists. In addition, he lectures and conducts workshops, chiefly on bioethics, and is the author of numerous articles and books, most recently, *Ethics of Health Care*, coauthored with Kevin O'Rourke, OP, and *Theologies of the Body: Humanist and Christian*.

IAN G. BARBOUR is Professor of Religion and Professor of Physics at Carleton College. He holds degrees in physics from Swarthmore College, Duke University, and the University of Chicago, as well as a degree in theology from Yale University. Dr. Barbour is a fellow of the National Humanities Center and a member of the Ethics and Values in Science and Technology Advisory Board of the National Science Foundation. He has received Fulbright and National Endowment for the Humanities fellowships and has been selected to give the Gifford Lectures (Aberdeen, Scotland) in 1989-1990 and 1990-1991. Dr. Barbour's publications include *Issues in Science and Religion* (1966); *Myths, Models and Paradigms* (1975); *Technology, Environment and Human Values* (1980); and articles in *American Journal of Physics*, *Journal of Religion*, *Christian Century*, and *Zygon: Journal of Religion and Science*.

JOSEPH A. BRACKEN, SJ, is Professor of Theology at Xavier University (Cincinnati), where he chaired the Theology Department from 1982-1985. He has taught at the Chicago Archdiocesan Seminary and at Marquette University. Fr. Bracken earned his Ph.D. in philosophy at the University of Freiburg, West Germany in 1968, under the direction of the noted phenomenologist Eugen Fink. His revised doctoral dissertation was published in the academic series *Symposion*, under the title *Freiheit und Kausalität bei Schelling* (1972). In addition, he has written two books: *What are They Saying About the Trinity?* (1979) and *The Triune Symbol: Persons, Process and Community* (1985). His articles appear in a number of academic journals.

FREEMAN J. DYSON is Professor of Physics at the Institute for Advanced Studies, Princeton University. He holds degrees in physics from Winchester College and Cambridge University. Dr. Dyson is a fellow of the Royal Society, London, and a member of the U.S. National Academy of Sciences and has served as chairman of the Federation of American Scientists. He is the recipient of the Hughes Medal of the Royal Society; the Max Planck Medal of the German Physical Society; the Robert Oppenheimer Memorial Prize; the Harvey Prize of the Technion (Israel); and the National Book Critics Circle Award for Non-Fiction. His recent publications include *Disturbing the Universe* (1979); *Weapons and Hope* (1984); *Origins of Life* (1986); and articles in *Scientific American* and *New Yorker*.

THOMAS M. KING, SJ, is Associate Professor of Theology at Georgetown University and holds degrees from the University of Pittsburgh, Fordham University, Woodstock College, and the University of Strasbourg. A spiritual director and former instructor of Jesuit novices, Fr. King is active in Campus Ministry at Georgetown. His books include *Sartre and the Sacred* (1974); *Teilhard's Mysticism of Knowing* (1981); and *Teilhard's Unity of Knowledge* (1984). His articles and book reviews have appeared in a number of journals, including *Teilhard and the Unity of Knowledge* (1983), which he edited. Fr. King organized the "Teilhard and the Unity of Knowledge" symposium (1981); has served as codirector of the "Cosmos and Creation" symposium since 1982; and has twice addressed an annual workshop on technology and theology.

JEROME J. LEJEUNE is Professor of Genetics on the Faculty of Medicine of the University of Paris and Executive Director of the Institut de Progenese. He holds degrees in medicine and natural science from the University of Paris. Dr. Lejeune is a member of numerous scientific societies in Europe, the United States, and Japan, including the Royal Society, London; the American Academy of Arts and Sciences; and the Pontifical Academy of Sciences.

He has received the *Prix Essec;* the Kennedy Prize; and the *Prix Cognacq-Jay* of the Paris Academy of Sciences and was named *Officier de l'Ordre National de Merite.* Dr. Lejeune, who discovered the cause of Down's Syndrome, has published widely in the field of cytogenetics, especially on the description and treatment of chromosomal abnormalities.

ERNAN MCMULLIN is the Director of the Program in History and Philosophy of Science at the University of Notre Dame. He holds degrees in physics and theology from Maynooth College and a Ph.D. in philosophy from the University of Louvain. Fr. McMullin is a fellow of the American Association for the Advancement of Science and the American Academy of Arts and Sciences. He has been awarded the Aquinas Medal of the American Catholic Philosophical Association; the Faculty Award for Distinguished Service of the University of Notre Dame; and the Centennial Medal of John Carroll University. His recent publications include *The Concept of Matter in Modern Philosophy* (ed. with introduction, 1978); *Newton on Matter and Activity* (1978); *Evolution and Creation* (ed. with introduction, 1985); and articles in *Zygon: Journal of Religion and Science, American Philosophical Quarterly,* and *Religion and Intellectual Life.*

PAUL M. QUAY, SJ, is Research Professor of Philosophy at Loyola University (Chicago). He holds an A.B. in classics from Loyola University, Licentiates in philosophy and theology from West Baden College, and a Ph.D. in physics for work in theoretical thermodynamics from the Massachusetts Institite of Technology. After a postdoctoral year in theoretical physics at Case Institute of Technology (Cleveland), Fr. Quay studied Ignatian spirituality and contemporary philosophy in France and Germany. At St. Louis University, he was Associate Professor of both physics and theology, spending two summers as consulting physicist for the National Bureau of Standards. Fr. Quay's current research lies in the areas of the theology of the spiritual life, the philosophy of science, and physics.

ROGER W. SPERRY is the Hixon Professor of Psychobiology at the California Institute of Technology. He holds degrees in English and psychology from Oberlin College and a degree in zoology from the University of Chicago. Dr. Sperry is a fellow of the American Academy of Arts and Sciences; a foreign member of the Royal Society, London; and a member of the Pontifical Academy of Sciences. He is the recipient of the Karl Lashley Award of the American

Philosophical Society; the Wolf Prize in Medicine; the Ralph Gerard Award of the Society for Neuroscience; and the Nobel Prize for Medicine and Physiology. Dr. Sperry's publications include a variety of scientific, theoretical, and philosophical essays in books and journals. Some of his recent articles are "Changed Concepts of Brain and Consciousness: Some Value Implications" (*Perkins Journal*); "The New Mentalist Paradigm and Ultimate Concern" (*Perspectives in Biology and Medicine*); and "Science, Values, and Survival" (*Journal of Humanistic Psychology*).

EDWARD O. WILSON is the Frank B. Baird, Jr., Professor of Science and Curator in Entomology, Museum of Comparative Zoology, Harvard University. He holds degrees in biology from the University of Alabama and Harvard University. Dr. Wilson is a fellow of the American Association for the Advancement of Science and the American Academy of Arts and Sciences and an honorary life-member of the American Genetic Association and the British Ecological Society. He has been awarded the National Medal of Science; the Leidy Medal of the Academy of Natural Sciences; the Distinguished Service Award of the American Institute of Biological Sciences; the Distinguished Humanist Award; and the Pulitzer Prize for General Non-Fiction. His major publications include *Sociobiology: The New Synthesis* (1975); *On Human Nature* (1978); *Genes, Mind, and Culture* (with C. J. Lumsden, 1981); and *Promethean Fire* (with C. J. Lumsden, 1983).

Cover Design: Douglas Been and Norman Carroll; Washington, D.C.
Typeface: Caslon
Typography: World Composition Services, Inc.; Leesburg, Va.